Fritz Reusswig, Lutz Meyer-Ohlendorf, Ulrike Anders

Partners for a Low-Carbon Hyderabad

A stakeholder analysis with respect to "Lifestyle Dynamics and Climate Change"

Emerging megacities
Dicussion Papers
Edited by Konrad Hagedorn, Christine Werthmann, Dimitrios Zikos, Ramesh Chennamaneni

Humboldt-Universität zu Berlin
Department of Agricultural Economics
Division of Resource Economics
Philippstr. 13, House 12
10115 Berlin

Tel.: +49 (0)30 2093 6305
Fax: +49 (0)30 2093 6497
www.agrar.hu-berlin.de/struktur/institute/wisola/fg/ress
www.sustainable-hyderabad.de

Contact: emerging.megacities@hu-berlin.de

The emerging megacities discussion papers are available at:
www.eh-verlag.de

ISSN print edition 2193-6927

Emerging megacities Discussion Papers are prepared by researchers working on topics in the realm of sustainable development in Megacities of Tomorrow, a research priority by the German Ministry of Education and Research (BMBF). The papers have been peer-reviewed by a board of external reviewers.
Views and opinions expressed do not necessarily represent those of the Division of Resource Economics.
Comments are highly welcome and should be sent directly to the authors.
We welcome contributions on any topics related to Megacities of Tomorrow. Further information on the submission procedure is given at:
www.sustainable-hyderabad.de/emerging-megacities

Reusswig, Fritz; Meyer-Ohlendorf, Lutz; Anders, Ulrike

Partners for a Low-Carbon Hyderabad
A stakeholder analysis with respect to "Lifestyle Dynamics and Climate Change"

Emerging megacities Discussion Papers, Volume 4/2009

ISBN/EAN: 978-3-86741-816-4

First published in 2012 by Europaeischer Hochschulverlag GmbH & Co KG, Bremen, Germany.

© Europaeischer Hochschulverlag GmbH & Co KG, Fahrenheitstr. 1, D-28359 Bremen (www.eh-verlag.de). All rights reserved.

Cover: Photo "Metropolis", ferendus (flickr). Creative Commons License

No part of this publication may be reproduced or transmitted, in any form or by any means, electronic, mechanical, photocopying, recording or otherwise, or stored in any retrieval system of nay nature, without the written permission of the copyright holder and the publisher, application for which shall be made to the publisher.

EHV

Partners for a Low-Carbon Hyderabad
A stakeholder analysis with respect to "Lifestyle Dynamics and Climate Change"

Fritz Reusswig[*,†], *Lutz Meyer-Ohlendorf*[†], *Ulrike Anders*[†]

May 2009

Abstract

This paper analyses the structure of local, regional and national stakeholders that might be relevant for a transition of Hyderabad into a low-carbon megacity. The main angle of the stakeholder selection in this report is defined by the leading question of our research: How do (local) lifestyle dynamics contribute to climate change, and how can lifestyle changes help to reduce local emissions and the vulnerability to global climate change? Our analysis reveals that climate change actually is a medium to low attention issue for the majority of stakeholders in Hyderabad (as in India in general). At the same time, the identified minority of individual or collective actors that actually do rate climate change higher on their agendas have the potential to form a critical mass for socio-ecological change in the city if (1) they improve their cooperation, if (2) institutional reforms in the urban space increase their impact, and if (3) they manage to align with a still 'silent majority' of stakeholders that by now rate climate change to be of minor relevance. The latter point is based on another key finding of our analyses: Actors with high structural power (based either on political, economic or network power) might be turned into potential 'allies' of a low-carbon strategy, if (1) they can interpret adaptation and mitigation options as new opportunities in their option space, (2) climate issues are more closely linked to sustainability issues, and (3) they perceive institutional reforms and stakeholder involvement as being beneficial for their daily operations. From these insights we derive some consequences for future pilot projects and policy advice.

Key words: *climate change mitigation, stakeholder analysis, stakeholder participation, Hyderabad, India*

---

[*] Corresponding author. Tel.: +49 331 288 2576. Email: fritz@pik-potsdam.de
[†] Potsdam Institute for Climate Impact Research (PIK), Research Domain Transdisciplinary Concepts and Methods, P.O. Box 60 12 03, 14412 Potsdam

1 Purpose of the Current Report

The current Hyderabad Megacity Project is–both from its funding and from its participant structure–a German undertaking. Nevertheless it tries to achieve progress in climate change related perceptions and actions in an Indian megacity. It is clear from the outset that this ambitious goal cannot be accomplished unless major actors in Hyderabad and elsewhere in India get involved and do actively support the project goals. In fact, we do assume that chances to adopt 'our' goals do only increase from near-zero if these actors do identify 'our' goals as their own ones—at least partially.

This requires a more or less 'clear picture' of the stakeholders one wishes to co-operate with. Who could be the 'partners for a low-carbon Hyderabad', and how could a co-operation look like? The current report tries to answer these questions from the particular perspective of the work package WP 2.1 ("Lifestyle Dynamics and Climate Change"). Other work packages will surely have other stakeholders in mind, and they will use other stakeholder analysis formats. With good reasons, given the basic intuition of the project as a whole that stakeholder co-operation in general and stakeholder analysis as a supporting tool must not be limited to one particular work package, but has to be detailed out and organised by each individual research team.

In our case, the stakeholder analysis does have a very special meaning. Lifestyle and consumption issues do not have a particular 'address' in a society. Neither is there a more or less clear cut (economic) sector called 'consumption', nor can we find a limited set of social actors shaping it. Even if one might think of 'the private households' as an economic sector or aggregated actor, one would still have to be aware of two caveats: (1) Private households differ significantly in their internal structure, e.g. with respect to size, income, educational level, economic assets, class and caste characteristics, spatial location etc. Most of these aspects clearly affect their actual (consumption) behaviour as well as their option space with regard to climate change mitigation and adaptation. A successful strategy to engage upper class households from, say, Jubilee Hills with respect to energy saving will most probably fail if applied to a poor household in one of Hyderabad's slum areas. As there is no single typical 'Hyderabad private household', any strategy to approach the aggregate 'household sector' in Hyderabad is either forced to develop differential strategies that take social differences into account—or almost surely doomed to fail. (2) Even a differentiated way to approach private households would not be able to grasp lifestyle and consumption issues in a society. Consumption as a social process and lifestyle as its structural driver and social location are both not confined to private household activities, but part of a wider set of actors and institutional practices. Who ever wants to analyse lifestyle and consumption issues in a structurally meaningful way does in fact have to talk about production and consumption systems; and it is only these systems that will become sustainable—or fail to achieve sustainability (Reusswig 2009).

For these two reasons the current report goes far beyond a decomposition of the urban household 'sector'. We have tried to embed the private households in a bigger picture including institutional aspects as well as influential other actors with the power to directly or indirectly shape the urban consumption process with respect to the overall project goals in a meaningful way.

It should be stressed that this report is not intended to be a final statement about how we perceive the stakeholders relevant to our WP. Stakeholder analysis is an ongoing process if one wishes to involve stakeholders in a research project, as we do. This implies that stakeholder analysis will be a continuing management task for the rest duration of the project.

The rest of this paper is organised as follows. We start with a short outline of methodological assumptions that had major influence on the choice of applied methods. (Chapter 2) We then give a scene-setting glimpse on the issue at stake: climate change from an Indian perspective (as far as we were able to reconstruct it) (Chapter 3). We then move to a brief overview of climate change as an issue for important political parties in India, as no pilot project and, particularly, no policy advice can ignore the political landscape of which actors are part (Chapter 4). A short look at how the Indian business community is prepared for climate change follows (Chapter 5). We then significantly broaden the scope of our analysis by looking at issues of social class and lifestyles more general in India. Besides addressing the particular profile of the actual work package, this move also serves as a complementary to the location of climate change in the political landscape (Chapter 6). We then present the major results of our empirical research work on major national and local stakeholders in India and Hyderabad and provide a participation planning diagram as a visualisation of the proposed project integration of our key stakeholders (Chapter 7).

2 Methodology

2.1 A Brief Review on Methods for Stakeholder Analyses

This review introduces preliminary assumptions that reflect the process of deciding which methods are best to be applied with respect to effectiveness regarding the project type and project objectives as well as efficiency by keeping in mind the available resources.

R. Edward Freeman, in the now classic text *Strategic Management: A Stakeholder Approach* (1984), defined a stakeholder as 'any group or individual who can affect or is affected by the achievement of the organisation's objectives' (1984: 46). Typical definitions of stakeholder from the public and non-profit sector literatures include the following variants:

- 'All parties who will be affected by or will affect [the organisation's] strategy' (Nutt and Backoff 1992: 439).

- 'Any person group or organisation that can place a claim on the organisation's attention, resources, or output, or is affected by that output' (Bryson 1995: 27).

- 'People or small groups with the power to respond to, negotiate with, and change the strategic future of the organisation' (Eden and Ackermann 1998: 117).

- 'Those individuals or groups who depend on the organisation to fulfil their own goals and on whom, in turn, the organisation depends' (Johnson and Scholes 2002: 206).

Having been developed in the business administration/organisation research community, these definitions display a clear bias towards organisations, especially business organisations. In that world, 'the stakeholder' has been a more recently emerging social role opposed (or complementary) to the more traditional role of, say, 'the shareholder' or 'the manager'. While these definitions and related analytical tools do not fully fit into the context of a research project addressing consumption and lifestyles in India, they still provide some useful insights (Bryson 2004). For our purposes, a 'stakeholder' is a person or organisation that either has the power to influence climate relevant consumption and lifestyle issues (structures, processes, outcomes) in Hyderabad, or is engaged in activities that bear the potential to bring about change (either in adaptation or mitigation measures). As nominally powerless actors (households, groups, organisations) may also be affected by climate relevant lifestyle and consumption issues, these are included in our definition.

While such a very broad and inclusive definition is faced with the problem of specification and operational practicability, it nevertheless adequately reflects the fact that both private and public corporations are more and more confronted with a growing complexity of problems to solve. Joseph (2006) for example highlights the fact that the involvement and participation of all the stakeholders such as the waste generators, waste processors, formal and informal agencies, non-governmental organisations and financing institutions have been a key success factor for the sustainable waste management.

This holds true for most public-private mixed problems that in addition display a clear global linkage, such as climate change. No single household or organisation is fully 'in charge', no single actor 'contains' the problem (Kettl 2002). It is only by co-operation of various different actors that adequate problem perceptions and solutions will come about. Put differently, we are moving into an era when networks of stakeholders are becoming at least as important, if not more important, than markets and hierarchies (Powell 1990), even if those networks are often operating in the 'shadow of hierarchy', or in the 'shadow of markets'.

A stakeholder analysis is no goal in itself. It is part of a research process, and should facilitate cooperation and participation, to build a "winning coalition" for strategic interventions and to enable for procedural justice, rationality and legitimacy (Bryson 2004: 24–26). However, stakeholder analyses are often conducted on an ad hoc basis and thus the identification and selection of stakeholders becomes arbitrary and might even "marginalise important groups, bias results and jeopardise long-term viability and support for the process" (Reed et al. 2009). In consequence, stakeholder analyses have been increasingly structured on a scientific basis and methods developed for practitioners.

Three stakeholder concepts can be distinguished: The *descriptive approach* is a prerequisite for further normative or instrumental stakeholder concepts. It describes the relation between the pivotal organisation or project and its stakeholders and can be realised through stakeholder mapping methods. It can be grounded on the empirical basis with a phenomenological orientation and give inputs to the normative or instrumental approaches. *Normative stakeholder theories* assume that understanding the different perspectives and conflicting interests of the stakeholders is crucial and an environment of "intersubjective validation" is necessary to induce change towards sustainability. The stakeholder analysis can contribute to this communication process. *Instrumental stakeholder approaches* are more pragmatic and aim to understand how organisations, projects and policy-makers can identify, explain, and manage the behaviour of stakeholders to achieve desired outcomes (see Figure 1) (Reed et al. 2009: 1936).

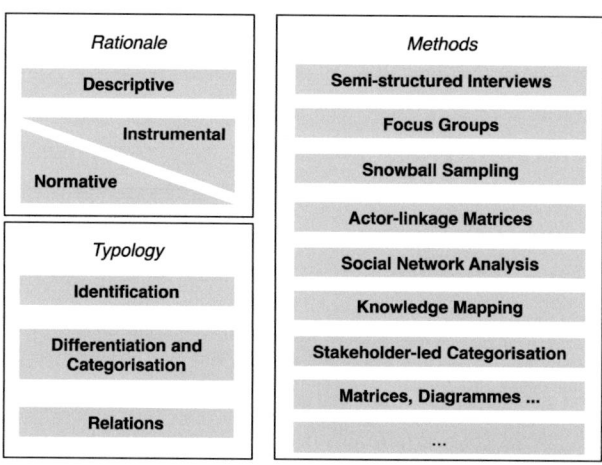

Figure 1: Rationale, typology and methods for stakeholder analysis
Source: Based on Reed et al. (2009)

For the purpose of the Hyderabad Megacity Project, the instrumental stakeholder approach seems most promising, because the analysis identifies how stakeholders are related to the project's objectives and it aims at a strategic management of stakeholder relations. It can increase participation and involvement, transform relationships, increase trust and understanding and finally lead to ownership of the processes in accordance with the objectives (Reed et al 2009: 1936). As pilot projects (situated and limited interventions) in Hyderabad as well as policy advice in a more general sense are among these goals, we had to focus on agency and engagement.

Based on these assumptions we analysed stakeholders with respect to two basic questions: (1) Which stakeholder is relevant/powerful enough to support the project goals, especially to mainstream energy and climate issues? (2) Which stakeholder is (intrinsically) interested in or committed to energy and climate issues? These two aspects are related, but divergent. An actor A may well be actively engaged with energy and climate issues in the urban context, but still lacks significant power as compared to others. On the other hand, we find a lot of structurally powerful actors that would be indispensible for putting forward low-carbon lifestyles in Hyderabad, without seeing them actively engaged in climate change or energy smart activities. These might rank low on their agendas, but without their change of priorities the overall issue cannot be moved ahead.

2.2 Operational Guideline for the Project

This operational guideline serves to facilitate the application of stakeholder analysis in other megacities' contexts. Figure 2 provides an overview of the applied methodical steps.

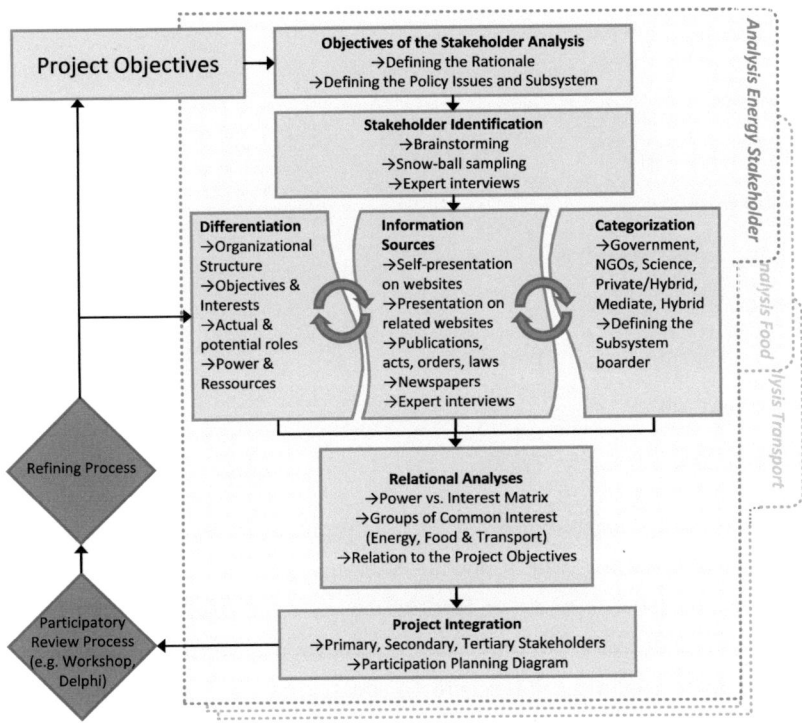

Figure 2: Operational guideline and methodical steps
Source: Based on a draft, kindly provided by Christian Kimmich, Humboldt-University, Berlin. Division of Resource Economics

2.2.1 Definition of Rationale, Policy Issues, and Subsystems

The rationale for the stakeholder analysis is given by the project goals on the one hand and the fact on the other that any attempt to improve energy efficiency and to reduce the carbon footprint of Hyderabad has to co-operate with elected and/or administratively responsible agencies, with the business sector, and with civil society in general. This requirement follows from legal, ethical and pragmatic considerations.

Our particular research issue is on energy consumption and lifestyles in the context of climate change. As mentioned, there is no clear-cut policy issue 'consumption and lifestyle' that would match the project goals in a one-to-one manner. Instead, lifestyle and consumption issues are crosscutting and require interdisciplinary efforts from the side of the scientists, and multi-facet and multi-stakeholder approaches with respect to the urban society.

There are, though, various existing policy issues that our research goal is related to and thus has to take into account:

- Energy policy
- Pollution control
- Housing policy
- Food and health policies
- Transportation policy
- Infrastructure and urban planning
- Educational policy
- Consumer Policy

These policy issues are implemented in various political subsystems of Hyderabad as a nested hierarchical system.[1] The following analysis tries to reflect this. In order to do so, we perceive the urban society of Hyderabad as a multilayered system with nested hierarchies and more or less autonomous sub-systems. The term 'autonomy' does refer to the fact that modern societies tend to create specialised and more or less independently operating areas of communication and action, following their own 'logic', with more or less loose couplings to other subsystems. Some sociologists (e.g. Niklas Luhmann) tend to 'exaggerate' the relative autonomy of social subsystems. We rather follow a more moderate view (cf. Münch 1996) that takes mutual interactions of these subsystems into account.

The subsystems we have been working with in our stakeholder analysis are rather broad, but enable us to cover a wide range of possible stakeholders in the first place. A finer selection had to follow. Our broadly defined subsystems are:

- Economy
- Politics

---

[1] This means that despite of our focus on Hyderabad we will of course have to take the multilayered political and institutional system of India and Andhra Pradesh into account. Many of the policy areas mentioned are not decided about by Hyderabad stakeholders, but at the state or Union level.

- Civil society

- Science and education

- Mass media

There is no doubt that stakeholders from the economic subsystem do play an important role when it comes to use energy more efficiently and to cut emissions (total or per unit of output). After having been perceived as more or less problematic social entities in the early phase of India's independent development, Indian cities have received particular attention since the early 1960s. Today, they are regarded as 'growth machines' with substantial regional growth effects. Megacities in particular do also have relevance for the national economy (Dholakia 2009, Sridhar 2006). While only 1.7% of the Indian population live in Mumbai, the city's economy generates 16% of India's GDP (Satterthwaite 2005). Hyderabad plays a key role in the region, and its IT and pharmaceutical industries have Indian-wide relevance.

Lifestyle and consumption related issues cannot be resolved by the individual consumer or at the household level exclusively. Sustainability in general and climate friendly consumption patterns in particular require changes along the lifecycle of products, which requires the cooperation of actors along the whole value chain. In developing countries, this value chain is particularly heterogeneous and fragmented in economic and social terms. On the one hand, we see businesses involved that operate on a global scale, meeting global competition standards, and implementing more or less the same internal business rules as their counterparts in the developed world. The Indian IT industry is a clear case in point here. On the other hand, one of the competitive advantages of the economies in developing countries is their relatively low wage level—especially, but not exclusively in areas of qualified labour. We thus find that even products that are competitive on world markets involve economic actors that can be small, if not marginalised in some respect. This holds even more for the ensemble of the local economy, where the contribution of the poor in many industry and service activities is indispensable. This heterogeneity of the economic subsystem is thus a challenge for a stakeholder analysis, but dealing with it also is a precondition for covering the relevant aspects for lifestyle and consumption issues.

It goes without saying that the political subsystem has to be part of a stakeholder analysis. Many boundary conditions for urban life are defined by politics, and many goods and services with climate relevance are provided by political actors (e.g. electricity, water). This holds true even after various waves of liberalisation in India since 1991.

Sometimes it seems as if the term 'governance' as a substitute for 'government' has been used to underpin a neoliberal ideology of liberalisation and privatisation. These aspects dominated the discourse of the 1990s. Today, especially after the recent crisis, which started in the financial sector, the role of the state and of government must be viewed in a different light. It is true that the political system in India is perceived by many as inefficient, overly bureaucratic, and corrupt. India ranks low in the international Corruption Perception Index (CPI) provided by Transparency International. However, the answer to this can, at least in our view, not be simply a switch mode and expect better governance from the private sector, especially when the provision of public goods or private goods in a highly unequal social setting is concerned. Instead, government reform seems to be an inevitable component of 'good governance'.

> *Changes in the urban environment depend on strategies adopted by the government, changes in environmental legislation and the stricter enforcement of existing legislation, the demand for better living conditions by urban residents, as well as the ability of local authorities to perform their functions, including partnership with other actors.* (Vira and Vira 2005: 52)

These remarks are necessary in order to understand our approach and the scope of political stakeholders we have included in this analysis. This is additionally reinforced by the crosscutting nature of climate change adaptation and mitigation for urban governance (Satterthwaite 2007).

Civil society does play an important role, especially in India after the reforms of the 1990s. Various political acts and concrete policies (e.g. the Right to Information Act[2]) have helped to empower civil society actors in order to put forward their views and interests. While India also is home of nation-wide NGOs, some of which do have international affiliations (e.g. Greenpeace India), the vast majority of NGO activism is located 'on the ground' in cities and regions. This holds also true for environmental NGOs, which come first to one's mind when climate and energy issues are key. Nevertheless, the scope of this sector is much larger for us, as we try to frame climate issues in the wider context of sustainable development—an area where many more activists and organisations are underway.

---

[2] The Right to Information Act 2005 was enacted by the Parliament of India giving citizens of India the right to access to records of any public authority. The Act also requires every public authority to computerise their records for wide dissemination and to proactively publish certain categories of information so that the citizens need minimum recourse to request for information formally.

Science and education as a subsystem have been selected because of the fact that climate change is a highly scientifically mediated domain of research. It is difficult if not impossible to attribute, for example, weather extremes to anthropogenic climate change by lay people. On the other hand, without scientific accuracy it is not possible to make these links between everyday life and the global climate system explicit in a serious and credible manner. This is why science and education are important subsystems for us. In addition, local scientific organisations such as universities provide an indispensible resource for doing research on the ground.

The mass media finally are a relevant subsystem as they help to create the public sphere in a society, communicating events and providing interpretation schemes for all kinds of political and other issues. In addition, next to their information function, the mass media entertain and influence the consumption choices of individuals, which also make them relevant to our WP.

2.2.2 Identification and Description of Stakeholders

The identification of stakeholders has to be seen as an iterative process that continues throughout the analysis. However, there is always the danger that relevant stakeholders may be accidentally omitted, but on the other hand it is often not possible to consider each and every one of them (Reed et al. 2009: 1937). Megacities are nodal points of organisational interaction from the local up to the international level. The sheer number of actors directly or indirectly shaping the urban consumption process significantly challenges adequate stakeholder sampling. Therefore, we are fully aware that any such analysis undertaken in limited time will probably miss important stakeholders, especially in a city as large and heterogeneous as Hyderabad (or in a country as India). We thus do not assume this report to be a final statement.

On the other hand, the context of a Megacity alleviates the collection of information with regards to potential actors, because most of the organisations working in the urban context have sufficient material at hand, mostly even available on their web pages. Nevertheless, a good starting point was to conduct interviews with local experts or project partners from the pilot project phase not only to collect a number of contact details to potential stakeholders through this snow-ball sampling method, but also gain insights into the local discourse on climate change and learn to understand the role of different actors in the discourse (cf. Reusswig et al. 2009). In addition, brainstorming of existing contacts together with project partners and researchers from other work packages were conducted to extend the list and fill the gaps in a puzzle of various relevant actors.

This bare list of stakeholders was the basis to collect accessory information via web research such as contact details, links to other organisations, duties of the organisation, its institutional profile, used (regulatory-) instruments and communication devices, as well as the organisations role with respect to climate change mitigation and adaptation. Through this web research it was possible to identify further relevant stakeholders mentioned on the web.

2.2.3 Categorisation and Differentiation

This comprehensive information data base was then reviewed and discussed by the team of WP 2.1 and served as the basis for the further categorisation and differentiation process of all identified stakeholders (see Table 1). Analytical categorisations can at best be carried out within the team of researchers based on the review of the information database and their own observations (Reed 2009: 1938). However, even though some of the following steps involve a rating in numbers, it provides statistical results that are based on the perceptions of the involved researchers. The comparing of stakeholders during the categorisation process and the facilitation of discussion of results reduces the danger of bias. For a first comprehensive categorisation, we applied a scheme that addresses the following aspects:

- **Power.** We distinguished three forms of power: (1) political power, (2) economic or market power, and (3) network based power.[3] The latter refers to social networks (or social capital) as well as to the ability of an actor to mobilise public attention (e.g. via the mass media). The three dimensions of influence of each stakeholder was discussed within the team of WP 2.1 and noted on a flip chart. This was helpful during the process of rating in order to compare with and refer to other afore categorised stakeholders. Each dimension of influence was rated between 1 and 5, with 1 representing the lowest and 5 representing the highest possible categorisation.

- **Relevance of climate change for the organisation.** This categorisation refers to the relevance of the issue of climate change for the organisation according to

---

[3] By starting with 'power' we wanted to counter the tendency of some stakeholder analysis in the context of governance studies to neglect power and power differentials as a central characteristic of stakeholders (Hust 2005). By differentiating between economic (or market), political and network power we wanted to acknowledge the social differentiation of modern societies in different subsystems with different resource bases, different modes of power acquisition and use.

the organisation's profile. Significance was differentiated in a qualitative manner as either 'high', 'medium', or 'low' (the same for all following aspects).

- **Actual role for climate change mitigation.** Here, the actual involvement of the organisation in climate change mitigation was categorised to highlight those organisations that may have a relatively high interest in the project's objectives.

- **Potential role in climate change mitigation.** This categorisation was rather estimated by the team of researchers by taking into consideration the organisation's potentially growing interest due to increasing awareness and capacity building measures through the project.

- **Actual role for climate change adaptation.** Here, the actual involvement of the organisation in climate change adaptation was categorised to highlight those organisations that may have a relatively high interest in the field of adaptation.

- **Potential role for climate change adaptation.** This categorisation was again rather estimated by the team of researchers by taking into consideration the organisation's potentially growing interest due to increasing awareness and capacity building measures through the project.

- **Assessment of the organisation's areas of interest.** In our analysis we also asked for the organisation's interest in one or more areas of the project's objectives, viz. energy, food/health, and/or transport/mobility (yes and no).

- **Pilot project role.** This category is based on the project's objective to promote pilot projects in the field of energy conservation and climate change mitigation. It is based on the researcher's judgment in how far the organisation may be able to contribute to implementing pilot projects in Hyderabad.

- **Policy advisory role.** Here, we took into consideration in how far the organisation would be able to play a role in policy advisory.

In a further step we discussed the outcome of this first categorisation and mapped stakeholders according to the power versus interest grid (see Figure 3; cf. Bryson 2004: 30), with the result of four categories of stakeholders: players who have both an interest and significant power; subjects who have an interest but little power; context setters who have power but little direct interest; and the crowd which consists of stakeholders with little interest or power. Besides helping to determine which players' interests and power bases must be taken into account in order to address the objectives of our project, it provides some information on how to convince stakeholders to change their views

(Bryson 2004: 31). Bryson also states that "the knowledge gained from the use of such a grid can be used to help advance the interests of the relatively powerless" (Bryson et al. 2002, cited in Bryson 2004: 31).

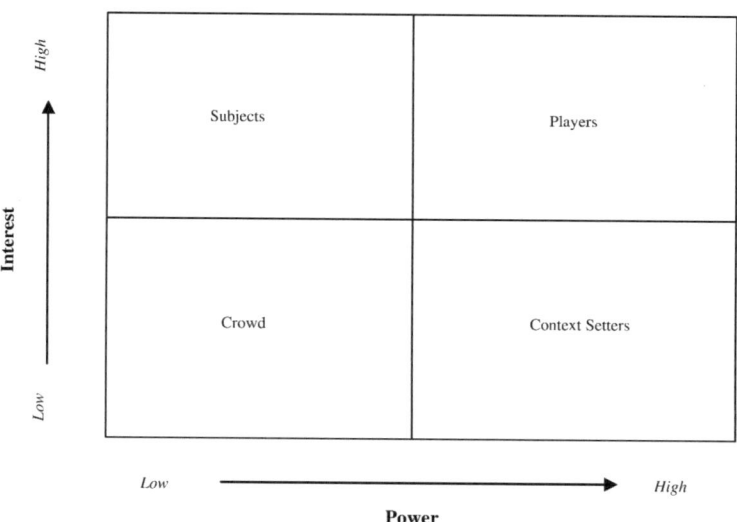

Figure 3: Power vs. interest grid
Source: Bryson (2004: 30)

Moreover, the analysis of power versus interest is a potent tool to help highlight coalitions to be encouraged or discouraged (Bryson 2004: 31). The large number of relevant stakeholders working in Hyderabad highlights the fact that it is crucial to promote cooperation based on common interests. To bring to light different interest groups with respect to the project's objectives, we highlighted all those stakeholders that work in the fields of energy, transport/mobility, and/or food respectively. The so obtained visualisation of three different interest groups (see Figure 6–8) facilitates addressing different stakeholders according to their interests and helps to identify potential actors with regard to winning coalitions for the project.

An outstanding crosscutting issue for the overall project is *capacity building* in Hyderabad. It is clear that any stakeholder analysis will have to focus on 'players'. Their high interest in our issues, combined with their power, predisposes them to be the primary stakeholder group for a science project. However, 'subjects' and 'context setters' are also interesting and important, as they either are actually attuned to the issue at stake (climate change), even if powerless ('subjects'), or would have a large potential impact due to their power despite actually lacking interest ('context setters'). But even 'the crowd' is relevant for us, as we assess a majority of private households as well as private or public organisations to both rank climate change relatively low on their agendas and to lack significant power for change. Nevertheless, as only aggregate effects of consumption and lifestyle changes, executed by a critical mass of consumers and citizens will bring about systemic changes (e.g. reduction of Hyderabad's GHG emissions or at least a limitation of its BAU growth), we did include them in our analysis.

If the differentials in power and interest of various stakeholders are taken into account, it becomes clear that the overall project goal of capacity building does mean different things to different stakeholders. Based on the differentiation between players, subjects, context setters, and the crowd, we tried to flesh out different variants of capacity building, which would be more suitable to these different groups.

- **Mainstream and connect:** 'Players' are powerful and interested, but often lack coordination and cooperation—which in part is a consequence of their high power. Powerful actors often tend to assume that they do not need to cooperate and align their interests and views with others, especially less powerful actors. We thus find it appropriate and necessary to direct capacity building towards more coordinated efforts.[4] By 'mainstreaming' we would like to refer to the fact that the crosscutting issue of climate change finds itself fragmented across the political and administrative sub-branches of many—even in general powerful—actors.

- **Connect and empower:** Among the group of 'subjects' are rather those stakeholders that have a great interest in one or the other project's objectives, but lack the power to exert their influence. These stakeholders are likely to increase their influence through improved cooperation with other stakeholders with common or similar interests. Therefore, capacity building measures can aim to facilitate cooperation and the establishment of winning coalitions.

- **Inform and empower:** Despite lacking interest and power, the 'crowd' shouldn't be neglected as they are still part of the overall picture of stakeholder interaction and as they may have certain knowledge and contacts relevant for the project. For instance, CHATRI was identified as a primary stakeholder for the pilot project phase due to their significant expertise in the field of urban slum development.

---

[4] According to Vira and Vira (2005), urban environmental policy in India lacks coherence between national, state and urban levels, as well as real power of local authorities when it comes to implementation.

CHATRI has little power as e.g. compared to TERI, but knows the local conditions and has important knowledge in working with the urban poor.

- **Inform and involve:** The most challenging task has to be seen in involving major 'context setters' who have the power to bring sighted changes, but lack the interest to do so due to various reasons. Often it is simply a lack of awareness that could be changed through capacity building measures. Given the high power and low interest structure of these actors, a simple provisioning with information will not suffice. Active involvement of those actors can only be gained once this information is made salient in terms of linking it to the specific operational conditions of these actors.

2.2.4 Project Integration

In order to support the development of strategic interventions for the case of Hyderabad in respect to the project's objectives it was necessary to create understanding of political feasibility based on the potential roles of certain stakeholders (cf. Bryson 2004: 32). The foregoing analytical steps served to depict stakeholders' interests, both separately and in relation to each other. This serves as a basis for further differentiation of stakeholders with respect to their roles for the entire work package. It is crucial to define all those who are supposed to get directly involved in the proposed intervention as *primary stakeholders*. *Secondary stakeholders* are all those who rather play a subsidiary role as they are e.g. connected with key actors or exert their influence on them (Jepsen and Eskerod 2008; GTZ 2001: 14). The definition of primary stakeholders is an important step that significantly builds on the foregoing analysis process. However, as important as such qualifications (primary, secondary) are from a pragmatic point of view, they must not be perceived as a final word. Neither do they hold with respect to all aspects or situations during the course of a project. Many 'secondary' stakeholders are crucial for the success of the project in a particular aspect, and often coalition building needs the integration of different stakeholder groups. In addition, experience in other projects shows that sometimes a good cooperation, based upon mutual interest and understanding, between a project and a 'secondary' stakeholder turned out to be more productive than a bad cooperation with a 'primary' one. This all sums up to the statement that while accepting stakeholder ranking for pragmatic reasons, we will not treat this initial categorisation as cast in stone.

Ultimately, all gained results coalesce in a *final participation planning diagram* that not only visualises the field of directly and indirectly involved actors. It also facilitates to bring out first hypotheses on differing influence on the project's objectives and it helps to keep in mind existing interrelationships between certain stakeholders (see Figure 10).

3 Climate Change from an Indian Perspective

From a Western point of view, chances to achieve this identification with the Megacity project goals seem to be quite high at a first glance: (1) The global community of climate and climate impact scientists more or less agrees that climate change is a real concern already now (and especially in the coming decades), as has been very powerfully revealed by the latest report of the Intergovernmental Panel on Climate Change (IPCC) in its Fourth Assessment Report (IPCC 2007). (2) The same community widely agrees upon the general finding that the most severe impacts of climate change will occur in the countries of the developing world, of which India is an important part. A natural interest in both adaptation to climate change and to mitigation policies at a global level thus seems to be a reasonable assumption. (3) For the case of India, a more or less symbolic aspect adds to the former two: The current head of IPCC is an Indian, Prof. Dr. Rajendra Pachauri, and he was—together with former U.S. Vice President Al Gore—awarded with the Nobel peace award in 2007. A more substantial aspect behind this more symbolic one is the fact that India is home of many first class research institutes that address climate change issues in various aspects; the Delhi-based Energy and Resource Institute (TERI), of which Prof. Pachauri is the director, being only a prominent example.

Nevertheless, aligning worldviews and interests between Western and Indian perceptions of climate change, is not an easy task as it might seem. From an Indian viewpoint, the dominant problem with climate change is that it has been—and still is—mainly caused by consumption and production patterns of the industrialised countries. In addition, India's carbon intensity—i.e. the amount of CO_2 emitted into the atmosphere in relation to the aggregated economic output (measured as Gross Domestic Product, GDP)—is also relatively low and slightly improving over time, ranging at 0.4-0.3 kg of CO_2 per Dollar GDP, which is about the value of EU 15, but much beyond the U.S. (0.6 kg) or China (0.7 kg) (IEA 2006).

Given the very low per-capita emissions of an average Indian (about 1.02 metric tons of CO_2 per year as compared to a world average of 4.25 tons, or to about 10 tons in the EU and 20 tons in the U.S.; GOI 2008), Indian stakeholders generally doubt both the necessity and the moral justification of talking about 'low-carbon lifestyles' in India—especially if Westerners do so. Why, so one can summarise their argument, should a country (or a city) reduce its emissions if the main emitters (a) are located in the developed world and (b) are faced with much less pressing development related problems? (Bhushan et al. 2008). The most prominent problem that Indian stakeholders generally put forward when it comes to doubt the justification of emission reductions is the widespread poverty in the subcontinent.[5]

While this situation highlights the necessity of Indian stakeholder involvement of any attempt to 'move' something with regard to climate policy in India, it at the same time underlines the difficulty to do so. And it reveals that the purpose of any stakeholder analysis in the context of lifestyle changes not only has the task to 'screen potential allies', but also—and even more so—needs to identify the world views and argumentation patterns of partners in a *dialogue* about climate change. This in a way describes both the general strategy and the spirit in which our research has been undertaken.

Fortunately, and this is also an important finding, discussing climate change with local/national stakeholders in Hyderabad and India in general is by no means an attempt in putting forward a 'Western agenda', at least not in principle. Most studies, both from international and from Indian scientists, reveal that climate change will affect the subcontinent in potentially disastrous ways (e.g. by triggering sea level rise and more severe droughts), and there is little doubt that the bulk of the burden will most probably be put on the shoulders of the urban and rural poor (Kelkar and Bhadwal 2007; Kolli et al. 2002; O'Brian et al 2004; Roy 2006).[6] There is ample reason for all those concerned with the future development of India, and the fate of the poor in particular, to take climate change seriously, as well as to think thoroughly about adaptation. We have found that many scientists, organisations and government bodies have the same perception, although—from our perspective at least—the process of mainstreaming adaptation to government policies still lacks the necessary vigour and coherence.

More astonishingly, though, many actors in India at various regional and political levels do in fact actively engage in climate change *mitigation* activities. At least from an outside observer point of view these activities—some of which will be portrayed in some more detail later in this report—seem an appropriate answer to the fact that India as a rapidly growing country—both with respect to the number of people it is home to as well as to the size of its economy—not only counts as a major emitter of Greenhouse

---

[5] About 26% of the urban (and 28% of the rural) population are assumed to be poor (according to the World Bank definition of living from less than 1 $US per day) (World Bank 2008).

[6] In the context of our Megacity Project, it is the task of WP 1 to identify the major impact paths of climate change for the Hyderabad region, as well as the major vulnerable groups.

Gases (GHG) already now, but will do even more so in the near future. Given its rapid economic growth, India will very soon loose one of the major arguments against Western countries: by 2030, the country will bypass Japan in terms of its accumulated emissions, and it will then most probably be the fourth largest emitter of GHG worldwide (Botzen, Gowdy and van den Bergh 2008: 572). With per capita emissions still below Western standards, India as a nation is nevertheless not only subject to climate change generated elsewhere, but at the same time part of the problem.

Our analysis suggests that even those stakeholders that do *not* accept the latter formulation want to be part of the climate *solution* though (Das, Mukhopadhyay and Pohit 2005). Climate and energy related activities, including various policies and programmes at all political levels, have been put forward. One driver of this development was the fact that—after some initial scepticism—the Government of India decided to utilise the Clean Development Mechanism (CDM) of the Kyoto Protocol as an important instrument to financially support energy efficiency and emission reduction projects, such as wind farms, biomass or waste based energy generation projects (Parikh and Parikh 2004). By now, the CDM is perceived as a potential instrument for win-win benefits, aimed towards local economic development and environmental improvements concomitant with controlling greenhouse gas emissions.

India is also playing a key role in international policy formation on greenhouse gas emissions. The country has strongly advocated that long-term greenhouse gas emissions should be the same per capita throughout the world—an equal human right to use the global commons.

The fact that the international community (especially the U.S., but also the EU and Japan) has increased its pressure on the Indian Government more recently (ToI, 29.6.2008) to accept internationally binding emission limitation goals can offer only a partial explanation.[7] A more careful look at these programmes reveals that most of them link climate issues with other problems of the country—such as rural development, environmental protection in general, energy security, or resource conservation. If we term those other aspects as elements of sustainable development, one can reasonably argue

---

[7] In fact, in the Indian case this pressure might even lead to increased opposition to binding climate goals. Many experts we have been talking to tend to believe that the situation in India is really different to the Chinese case, which for Indians is always a major landmark for orientation. Chinese climate policy initiatives can, at least to a higher degree, be traced back to the very sensitive reaction of leading Chinese (communist) politicians to international pressure, whereas India, as a long-standing democracy is a much more 'accepted' member of the international community, resulting in a somewhat higher self-esteem when it comes to turn down international claims that are perceived to violate Indian interests.

that many activities of stakeholders that in fact either improve energy efficiency or reduce GHG emissions by alternative energy sources are often at least as much framed under the heading of 'sustainable development' as under the heading of 'climate policy'.[8]

We assume this to be of major importance for the further course of our Megacity Project. It not only offers a strategic opportunity that enables Western scientists to align with Indian stakeholders. It also reflects an objective choice of Indian climate policy. As Shukla, Dhar and Mahapatra (2008) have demonstrated convincingly based upon climate and energy modelling, India as a whole can choose between two very different pathways of climate policy: One in which the energy sector is a deliberate target of interventions (such as carbon taxes and Carbon Capturing and Storage, CCS technologies), and one in which a multitude of policies aiming at the sustainable use of energy and other resources (e.g. due to substitutions or more efficient consumption of materials). Both policies result in more or less the same amount of avoided GHG emissions, i.e. can be termed effective climate policies.[9] But only the former is actually framed as 'climate policy', whereas the second much more deserves the title of a sustainability policy. The 'Carbon Tax' scenario focuses on the energy sector, and the relative price difference between renewable and fossil fuels is reduced by a carbon tax, which enables faster penetration of Renewables. Renewable energy sources do also penetrate through society, but for different reasons.

In a sustainable society, the co-benefits of renewable energy, as well as higher deployable potential and lower transaction costs due to cooperation among the stakeholders, propel the penetration of renewable resources. Such a low carbon transition would be accompanied by improved local environment and energy security, which are the key issues for a rapidly developing large economy like India. These issues would need to be addressed regardless of carbon mitigation. (Shukla, Dhar and Mahapatra 2008: 173)

---

[8] This is a strategic embedding that is by no means limited to the Indian situation, but can be found in many other developing country policies addressing climate change. The Caribbean Community Climate Change Centre (CCCCC), for example, located in Belmopan (Belize), uses sustainable development as a 'hook' in order to mainstream climate change issues (adaptation, mitigation) into existing social and political processes in the Caribbean context (Dr. Neville Trotz, CCCCC, personal communication).

[9] The so-called 'Carbon Tax' scenario results in a total amount of 62.6 billion t of avoided CO_2, whereas the so-called 'Sustainability Scenario' results in 59.3 billion t. The period under consideration in both scenarios is 2005 until 2050, a period in which India's Gross Domestic Product (GDP) is assumed to increase by 23.6 times. Emissions increase from 1,291 million t CO_2 in 2005 to 6,636 million t CO_2 in 2050 in the base case scenario. The cumulative emissions during the 45-year period (2005-2050) are 162.3 billion t CO_2.

The basic message from this modelling exercise is in fact encouraging: There are at least *two*, not only one single pathway(s) to a low-emission society in India.[10] This does have some implications for a stakeholder analysis in this context. (1) Stakeholders should be selected in view of a multitude of *different* pathways to a low-carbon society/city. (2) While it is crucial to have representatives from the power sector in the sample, one must not confine urban low-carbon strategies (and related stakeholder analysis) to actors and mechanisms of this sector. (3) It is crucial to keep the various links between energy/climate policies on the one hand and sustainable development policies on the other in mind. This holds for potential co-benefits of low-carbon policies as well as for the complex nexus between energy, climate, water, land use, poverty alleviation, and various other aspects of sustainable development. (4) Given the precarious role of explicit climate policy in the Indian context, it can be of crucial strategic importance to frame energy and climate issues in the wider context of sustainability issues. This also implies that stakeholders who—at a first glance—seem to have hardly any relation to climate change still can be of high relevance for a *de facto* low-carbon policy.

While it seems promising to link climate change issues to the overall framework of sustainable development (SD) (cf. Reddy and Assenza 2008, Srivastava 2006), one still has to ask how SD is perceived by stakeholders and how urban sustainable development in particular would be able to support adaptation and mitigation strategies.

Our interviews show that 'sustainable development' in the Indian context is by and large biased towards sustainable *rural* development. As understandable as this might be given the high economic and social relevance of agriculture and rural habitats in general for India, it is nevertheless a problematic link if the sustainable development of urban agglomerations is at stake. Given this bias between rural India and sustainability, the very notion of urban sustainability becomes problematic unless it can be shown how it can be incorporated in the urban context in a meaningful way—including meaningfulness for relevant stakeholders.

A comprehensive study of urban environmental sustainability issues concludes that sustainable urban management would have to include the following aspects (TERI 2009: IX-X):

- Presence of well-functioning infrastructure.

---

[10] According to Shukla, Dhar and Mahapatra (2008) both scenarios are feasible in economic terms, i.e. they do not assume prohibitively high mitigation costs.

- Existence of a legal framework that enables and empowers governments/departments to set up goals, create roadmaps, and carry out the necessary implementation measures.
- Presence of well coordinated institutional and governance mechanisms and unified bodies enabling implementation of integrated sustainability measures.
- Existence of strong political leadership and will.
- Setting of clearly defined goals and measurable targets and stage-wise review and monitoring of plans and targets with necessary updating wherever required.
- Implementation of a continuous, interactive and iterative multi-stakeholder participatory process involving both sectoral experts and general community throughout.
- Execution of demonstration projects to win public support and acceptance.
- Presence of sense of ownership and responsibility amongst citizens.
- Replication of successful initiatives by other cities.

It is clear almost *a priori* that no single city (or organisation within it) will meet all of these criteria at the same time. The important point for bringing about urban sustainability is to help moving core stakeholders in the right direction at various points at the same time. And it might also be helpful to analyse what specific asset or ability of a particular stakeholder might be used in order to compensate for some lacking capabilities in another domain.

We will try to mainstream climate change issues (adaptation, mitigation) in such a way that winning coalitions of stakeholders can arise. If necessary or appropriate—and this seems to be the case more often than not—we will have to link climate issues to urban sustainability, which broad goal again has to be specified according to domains and actors. The findings of the TERI study mentioned will serve as a guiding line to do so. In the wider context of the Hyderabad project, what has been termed the 'water-energy-resource nexus' is the core element of that mainstreaming strategy.

4 Indian Political Parties and Climate Change

For an outsider, India's political landscape is at least as diverse and hard to grasp as, say, its natural landscape; probably it is much more in-transparent. The following piece does thus not claim to be neither comprehensive nor complete. Its only purpose is to give a basic orientation of how political parties perceive climate change in order to locate our own goals in a rudimentary non-naïve way.

India has a multi-party system with predominance of small regional parties. National parties are those that are recognised in four or more states. But the political reality in many states and local communities are coined by a multitude of parties, and by multi-party coalitions. A typical Western (or even only European) approach to political parties is to sort them along a left-right gradient which turned out to be a rather stable element of political orientation for centuries now. However, even in Europe the emergence of Green political parties has challenged this view, as they not fully fit into it. But even if no fully analogue to European Green parties could have been identified by us, the European left-right gradient does not fully grasp the political reality of India. Endowed with regional differences that no single European country is experiencing, and with social and cultural fragmentations that are equally unique for European citizens, additional aspects have to be put forward.[11]

In India, almost 70 % of the whole population live in rural areas (UNDP 2007) and it is remarkable that this rural population still shapes the outcome of any election. Therefore, any environmental movement in India and its related discourse is still closely related to the question of economic development and poverty alleviation. For instance, the well-known Chipko movement in the 1970s, wherein villagers from present-day Uttarakhand hugged trees to prevent them from being cut, was a conservation movement, but also driven by the concern on the livelihood of the people (see results of discourse analysis).

The intricate, but sometimes conflict-prone connection between environmental issues and economic development represents an argumentation pattern that can also be asserted in the Indian party politics. Party manifestos of the four major national parties, the *Indian National Congress, INC* (leading party in the ruling coalition between 2004 and 2009 of the *United Progressive Alliance, UPA*), the *Bharatiya Janata Party, BJP* (leading opposition party in the *National Democratic Alliance, NDA*), the *Communist Party of India (CPI)*, and the *Communist Party of India, Marxist (CPI/M)*[12] show that the environment and climate change in particular plays a certain role during the 2009 national elections and it is remarkably treated with a quite strong consensus.

The coalition leader of the ruling *United Progressive Alliance*, UPA (2004-2009) – *Indian National Congress* (INC) – emphasises the *National Action Plan on Climate*

---

[11] Although no single European country reaches India's complexity, the European Union as a political body of its own does in fact offer better analogies.

[12] Unfortunately, both the Telangana Rashtra Samithi (the two major regional political parties in Andhra Pradesh) have released their party platform in Telugu, not in English.

Change (NAPCC) as its strong point and addresses climate change as a serious challenge. The National Action Plan is understood as an adequate comprehensive answer to it without compromising the overall objective of economic growth.

It is an acknowledgment of our responsibility to take credible actions within the overall framework of meeting the development aspirations of our people for higher economic growth and a higher standard of living. This action plan will be implemented in letter and spirit. (INC 2009: 18).

The National Action Plan emphasises the importance of technology transfer from the developed world and highlights sustainable technologies as the key to climate change mitigation in India. Moreover, the INC gives a strong argument for nuclear energy as a clean technology. Therefore, it is not a big surprise that the INC manifesto highlights the INDO-US nuclear deal as a matter of supreme national interest.

Remarkably, INC does not pledge for quantifiable reduction targets, neither in its party manifesto, nor in its NAPCC, arguing that India has very low per capita GHG emissions. The NAPCC only promises that its per capita greenhouse gas emissions will at no point exceed that of developed countries even as it pursues its development objectives (GOI 2008: 2). Therefore, NAPCC can be seen as a strategic concession to pressures from the UNFCCC Annex 1 parties. This and the other INC positions show how close environmental issues are coupled with other political agendas such as economic growth, technological development, energy security, and self-sufficiency.

The CPI follows on a similar vein arguing with India's existing reduction strategy against formal reduction targets:

> *While reducing emissions in our own and global interest, India must not succumb to pressures to compensate for historical damages caused by others. CPI will resist schemes to escape responsibilities through monetary payoffs or speculative exercises like carbon trading. India should insist on global emission cuts on the basis of equitable per-capita entitlements.* (CPI 2009)

CPI/M states a quite similar standpoint but is a little more specific by suggesting the control of GHG emissions through energy efficient technologies and effective regulation as well as through promotion of solar and other non-conventional energy sources. Other environmental issues are also mentioned in the manifesto of the CPI/M.

However, contrary to the INC stand the positions of both Communist Parties, CPI and CPI/M, taking a strong point against the Indo-US nuclear deal as ambassadors of India's Non-Aligned Movement:

The Manmohan Singh government betrayed its own Common Minimum Programme to forge a strategic alliance with the United States to sign the unequal Indo-US nuclear deal, thus undermining our independent foreign policy. (CPI/M 2009: 2)

The most specific party platform with respect to environmental issues for the 2009 national elections was released by the BJP. However, more specificity does not mean a differing argumentation pattern and economic growth and development of sustainable technologies stand at the core also for BJP.

The BJP will pursue national growth objectives through an ecologically sustainable pathway that leads to mitigation of greenhouse gas emissions. We recognise that containing global warming is essential to protecting life and security of people and environment. Mitigating the threat by building a low carbon economy is the biggest economic opportunity of the 21st century. As a matter of fact, BJP does not differ from the positions taken by the other parties with respect to India's role concerning global mitigation of climate change. BJP also insists on the promises made by the international community for technology transfer and additional financing since Rio (BJP 2009).

The BJP endorses the principle of "common but differentiated responsibilities", as enshrined in the UN Framework Convention on Climate Change. We look at 'Climate Change' in the context of the promises made by the international community for technology transfer and additional financing since Rio, which have remained unfulfilled. The BJP will actively pursue the transfer of critical technologies that can have a significant impact on reducing carbon emissions (BJP 2009).

With respect to nuclear energy, BJP highlights its important role in the development of India's strategic nuclear program and the nuclear tests in Pokhran-II and it emphasises the need of nuclear technologies for India, be it military or civilian. Nevertheless, BJP attacks the UPA driven Indo-US nuclear deal due its countervailing impact on India's strategic interests (BJP 2009).

In summary, the major national parties in India have a very common approach to tackle the problem of climate change. Economic development and growth is seen as a core theme in the Indian political discourse. Climate change is not taken as a stand-alone topic but rather serves as a cross-sectoral issue and it is treated with the promotion of technological development.

The differing positions on the Indo-US nuclear deal show that the parties have rather disparate policies, but it is remarkable that there is a quite strong consensus on the topic of climate change.

5 The Business Sector

As mentioned, the business sector is important when it comes to energy efficiency and emission reductions. The industry sector in India is a very energy intensive one (Ray and Reddy 2008). One important source for assessing the position of the Indian business community towards climate change is the KPMG (2008) study, based on interviews (April 2007) with 73 business leaders from a broad range of industries (energy, car manufacturing, metal, oil and gas etc.). Although no regional specification is given, it nevertheless gives a first overview of what the Indian business sector thinks and does about climate change.

According to a vast majority of managers, international pressure on India is perceived to be high. While the Indian economy getting increasingly integrated in global trade and business, the pressure from European Union and USA could get difficult to ignore. It is important to note that this international pressure is not received from a political, but from a genuine business perspective. For our project this would mean that chances for local cooperation are higher if the business corporation we will contact (e.g. for pilot projects) display a higher degree of international economic integration. This is true for Hyderabad's IT industry, and we will check it also for the pharmaceutical and other locally relevant industries (Kaschub 2007).

1 % of the business leaders do not believe in CC. 41 % say they fully understand the issue, know about their corporate carbon footprint, and have developed a strategy to reduce it. 42 % say they have a good understanding of CC, but still are in the process of developing a strategy. 16 % do not understand the issue well enough to dispose of a worked out strategy.

65 % of the interviewed business leaders think that India should take a leading role in acting on climate change, even if its low per capita emissions are considered. 35 % second to such a pro-active role only if other countries go ahead. Only 3 % believe that India should not take any action. Closer inspection, however, shows that the term 'India' by and large refers to 'the government'. Indian business leaders thus expect the Indian government to take a lead role in tackling climate change.

If asked about the risks that their businesses face with respect to global warming, 58 % name government regulation, ahead of physical impacts (51 %), loss of reputation in case of inaction (29 %), or litigation (18 %). The study results show that influence of employees, customers or investors is not a driving force behind firms' decision to respond to climate change. This is reflective of the lack of pressure that these stakeholder groups have exerted on this issue in India.

These results reveal that pressure from competitors, up- or downstream actors or the civil society is perceived to be less relevant than the expected regulation from the Indian government and from the international community. Companies and sectors that fail to adjust to a changing business environment created by laws and regulations face competitive disadvantages, while regulatory uncertainties make it difficult for companies to plan ahead.

If asked about the motivation to reduce the overall carbon impact of the company, 46% of the respondents named a benefit for the whole community, while 32% mentioned an increase in global trend to climate friendly business practices. 17% mentioned a growing market of low energy/carbon products and services, while 12% expected an enhancement of their brand image. Energy efficiency, clean technologies, and CDM opportunities are named as the three most important areas in which companies are planning or working towards exploiting business opportunities resulting from climate change.

20% of companies measure their complete carbon impact, while 14% restrict themselves to corporate GHG emissions. 30% only measure energy efficiency. 17 of the corporations do not measure at all, 12% plan to do so, and 3% don't know. Again, we can see a slight influence of the oversampling of the energy sector, where energy efficiency as well as GHG emission measurements are both a common practice. However, we found it astonishing that one fifth of the sample claim to calculate a total corporate carbon footprint.

The study concludes:

> *In summary, this study found that Indian businesses regard climate change as an important business issue. However, an appreciation of why it is important and how it can affect business appears to be relatively low. This, coupled with little stakeholder pressure, results in lack of structured approach to responding to climate change.* (KPMG 2008: 29)

Business risk is a function of both the objective risks a business (or business sector) is facing, and the degree of its preparedness. Even if the former is high, a high level of preparedness can turn it into a moderate total business risk. In order to prepare better, KPMG suggests various steps, including the measurement of the corporate carbon footprint, corporate carbon footprint scenarios, identification of business opportunities under a low carbon scenario, preparation and implementation of time bound action plans, the institutionalisation of a measurement and verification system, and the periodical reporting of progress to stakeholders.

6 Social Classes and Lifestyles

The dominant Western discourse on climate change displays a clear bias towards technological solutions, whereas consumption and lifestyle changes are put forward by many NGOs and some scientists. According to our assessment, there is no chance to achieve the necessary GHG reduction goals (with respect to a temperature stabilisation goal of 2 °C) without making substantial progress in both domains: technological changes in order to increase energy efficiency and to substitute fossil by renewable energy sources on the one hand, and consumption and lifestyle changes to either support and enable these technological changes, or to reduce overall energy consumption (Reusswig and Battaglini 2008). If lifestyle and consumption changes are not addressed, any gains in technological efficiency are simply being swamped by the sheer scale of rising aspirations and an increasing population. If everyone in the world lived the way Americans do, annual global CO_2 emissions would be 125 gigatons—almost five times the current level—by the middle of the century (Jackson 2008).

In the case of India, the same basic link between technology and lifestyle holds true. However, as noted in Chapter 2, India's situation is very different from the European or American one, given the low per capita emissions and its 'drivers', i.e. a comparatively low level of overall development—including endowment of GHG generating technologies—and a large, yet often poor population. Addressing consumption and lifestyle changes by simply applying European/American discourses and recipes without realising the different context are thus doomed to fail. This is in part reflected by our attempt to embed climate mainstreaming in urban sustainability issues. In addition, one has to positively relate emission reduction strategies with strategies to improve the livelihoods and quality of life, especially with respect to the urban poor. This would, for example, mean to design campaigns for substituting biomass burning in inefficient stoves by more efficient or clean ones that at the same time address issues like energy prices, energy security, time allocation (especially of women and girls), or indoor pollution.

At the same time, India does not equal poverty or the poor. Especially after its economic success since the reform period, the country has experienced a significant growth of its middle classes, complementing the traditional setting of upper and lower classes by a segment that adopts more modern (sometimes: Westernised) lifestyle and consumption patterns, very often more resource-intensive and wasteful ones, and thus, due to its growing size and share in India's social structure, contributes to growing overall and per capita emissions of the country as a whole.

In this chapter, we would like to expand our stakeholder analysis a little by addressing social class and lifestyle aspects. Stakeholders cannot only be classified according to their position towards an issue or their institutional roles. Especially if focusing on lifestyle and consumption issues, any stakeholder analysis does also have to account for a localisation of stakeholders in the social space of inequalities, or social class (Bourdieu 1987).

Despite a significant increase in public debates about the size and political orientation of the Indian middle classes after the economic reforms of the 1990s, this is by no means a new development. It can be argued that the middle classes have been the key drivers behind India's independence. Then the dominant members of the middle class, supported by many others who occupied positions of some authority in state and private sector institutions, set about building the modern Indian state. It was a time of idealism and of commitment to service to the nation (Varma 1998).

The social and political changes of the 1980s and 1990s, in which the middle classes were such significant actors, were associated, too, with a shift in their values. Varma (1998) laments that ideals of service gave way to ruthless individualism, that austere ways of life came to be replaced by consumerism, and that the values of the middle class, ironically, came to resemble those reflected in the self-seeking actions of the politicians they so much despised.

Even if India today is still a long way from having a fully liberal market economy, greatly increased consumption—if not actual 'consumerism'—and distinctive patterns of consumption that actually help define 'the middle class'—have become a prominent aspect of Indian society over the last 15 years or so.[13]

Many of our interview partners have indicated that the success story of India's economic growth since the restructuring of the 1990s does in fact make them feel proud of their country. The success of Indian enterprises and market segments—most prominently the IT industry and related services—is accompanied by cultural success stories, such as the growing global fan community for 'Bollywood' movies and contemporary Indian music. There is little doubt that post-reform India is on its way to a global superpower—a superpower that at the same time is characterised by many inner tensions

---

[13] At the same time, non-élite middle classes do not simply imitate Western lifestyles, but rather use new forms of media and goods consumption in order to layer them on top of their existing meaning and value systems, e.g. with respect to gender roles and stereotypes (Derné 2008).

and contradictions, with a large share of poor people as only one of them (Cohen 2001; Ganguly 2003; Mistry 2004).

This anecdotic evidence reflects a very serious underlying social process. Due to India's economic growth and transitions of its overall political economy, both social structures and their geographical distribution are rapidly changing. One of the most prominent examples of this change is the growth of the Indian middle classes. Estimates of its size clearly depend upon (and vary by) its definition (Fernandes 2006; Fuller and Narasimhan 2007; Sridharan 2004; van Wessel 2004). If 'class' was to supersede 'caste' in its meaning regarding social inequality, the emerging middle classes contributed much to this shift (Béteille 1996). Moreover, the size and the goals of the emerging middle class is part of a social discourse on India's new power and future development. Even if it is just "a small segment of urban upwardly mobile people that has provided the basis for the discursive production of the image of 'the new middle class'" (Fernandes 2006: 89), this public discourse not only reveals the developmental desires, but also reflects the shifting social realities of urban India. Not only the size and composition, but also the evaluation of the social and environmental effects of the emerging middle class is disputed. On the one hand, a growing middle class is assumed to have different positive implications for the Indian society, such as growing entrepreneurship, savings and investment, and demand for goods and services. A growing demand for political participation is usually attributed to the middle classes, leading to improved checks and balances and, eventually, an increased probability of improved policy outcomes. Indirectly, a growing and prospering middle class can increase the economic and political power of the whole nation (Bhalla 2004).

On the other hand, growing demand for consumer goods, such as cars, homes, household appliances, etc., leads to increased resource consumption (water, energy, space, matter...) and greenhouse gas emissions (Gadjil and Guha 1995; Mawdsley 2004). Consumerist middle classes are accused of lacking social values and insufficiently subscribing to governmental pro-poor policies (Harriss 2005; Varma 1998). Bangalore may be regarded as the iconic city of India's modernity, as well as of its multi-facetted middle class (Dittrich 2009). The IT branch as a highly visible cornerstone of India's new middle class (Fuller and Narasimhan 2007; Upadhyay 2004) is especially relevant for Hyderabad, a city that has tried to modernise especially in the IT sector, with 'Cyberabad' being the core spatial expression of this development strategy.

When it comes to future prospects and possible scenarios, the self-perceptions and expectations of people are at least as important as their objective social situation—following the old sociological truth that "If men define situations as real, they are real in their consequences." (cf. Merton 1995) Asked about how people defined their social positions, most lower income people do not answer 'the poor' or 'the working class', but rather 'the middle class'. This indicates the degree to which even members of the poorer social classes want to see themselves as middle class.[14]

The more India develops, the less the country can be 'defined' by its urban and rural poor—as important as they may remain being. While demonstrative consumption policies—or, to use a term coined by Veblen (1899), 'conspicuous consumption'—may also occur among rural (Jha 2007) and urban poor (Kumar and Aggarwal 2003), the main social stratum that consumes and publicly demonstrates its membership with the global consumer class (Myers and Kent 2003) are the middle classes (Ahmad and Reifeld 2002; Fernandes 2006, 2007; Shukla, Dwivedi and Sharma 2004; Sridharan 2004). The emerging vision of a 'consumerist India' runs well against the visions of self-reliance and frugal lifestyles that have a long-lasting tradition in India's culture and politics—with Mahatma Gandhi being a very powerful historical representative (cf. Kapur 1982; Kothari 1974; Rajni 1998), while other observers of India's recent path to modernity and liberal economic reforms highlight the cross-fertilisation of a rising middle class and the growing international relevance and power of India as a nation (Cohen 2001; Kalam and Rajan 1998).

The analytical assessment of the role and socio-economic relevance of the Indian middle classes cannot be separated from more general issues, such as liberal reforms of the 1990s, the role of state policies, or India's position in a globalising world (Deshpande 2003; Fernandes 2007; Jenkins 1999; Nilekani 2009; Oommen 2004). Much of the debate has focused on the size of the middle class–whether it is, say, 50 million or 150 million or 250 million–and the criteria to be used in drawing boundaries. Political critics of liberalisation tend to both downplay the share of the middle class in India's social structure and to criticise its presumed 'predatory consumerism', while proponents of liberalisation tend to overestimate its size and to downplay its negative impacts on society and natural resources.

While many market-oriented research defines 'middle class' basically via income (e.g. MGI 2004, see Figure 4), more sociologically oriented researchers focus on structural

---

[14] Very similar to China, where even the official rhetoric of the Communist Party has approved to middle class values. However, China has up to now managed to move more people out of poverty than India.

characteristics such as occupational position or cultural capital (Béteille 2001; Deshpande 2003; Sridharan 2004). Nevertheless, the basic quantitative findings of both types of research converge. Sridharan (2004) for example calculates for the late 1990s a total share of 25.81 % middle class in the widest sense and of 5.7 % if defined very narrowly ('elite middle class'). Market research by McKinsey Global Institute (MGI 2007) comes up with the following assessment, combined with a scenario for the future development of income classes.

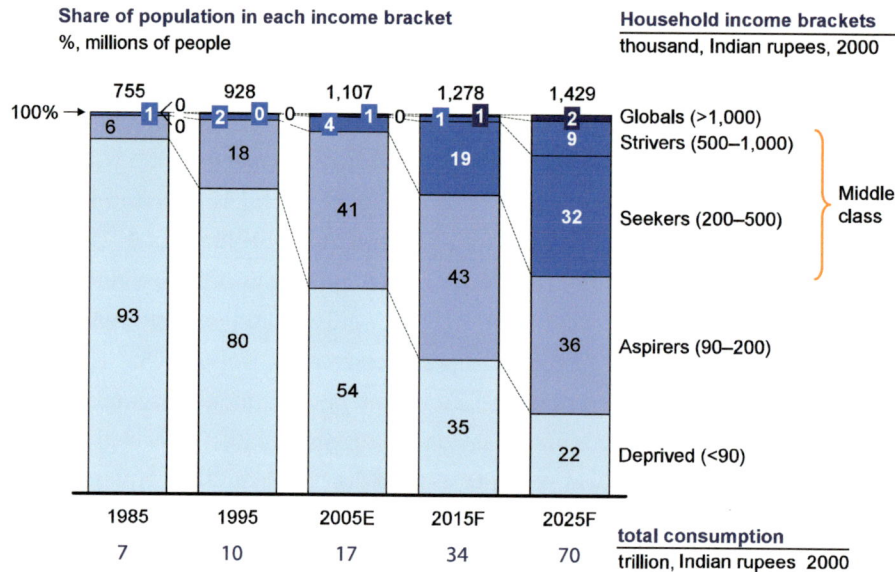

Figure 4: Change of income distribution in India 1985-2025 and total consumption
Source: MGI (2007: 12)

According to this study, the Indian middle classes comprised the two segments 'seekers' (200-500 thousand Rs. household income per annum) and 'strivers' (500-1,000 Rs.), together accounting for 5 % of the population in 2005.[15] By 2025, this middle class is assumed to comprise 41 % of the Indian population. Of course this is a scenario, and the most crucial variable is the growth rate of the Indian economy, as MGI notes explicitly. The scenario pictured above assumes an average annual growth rate of 7 to 8 %; slower

---

[15] 200 thousand rupees translates into 3,021 €, or 252 € per month, and 8 € per day. If we assume the average household size of 4 persons, the lower threshold of middle class membership is equivalent to 2 € per capita per day—slightly higher than the 2 $ per capita per day threshold of a wider poverty definition by the World Bank. Of course, one would also have to take the Indian price levels into account, as well as the fact that 2 € look different if the social environment is similar rather than much richer.

growth would slow down the growth of the middle classes. Given the actual performance and political planning in India, this growth is ambitious, but by no means unrealistic.[16] The effects of the actual economic crisis, which has also affected the Indian economy, are not accounted for. We will have to observe in the near future how this affects Hyderabad.

As important as the middle classes have—and will—become in terms of both consumption and politics, their much-debated rise must not obscure the fact that India is a poor country, if measured in the share of people with low incomes. Even according to MGI (2007), a market research institute that could easily be conceived as 'exaggerating' the size of the middle classes for business reasons, the lower classes in India account for 95 % of the population ('aspirers' and 'deprived').

Looking at stakeholders in India without taking castes into account would be sociologically naïve, and practically misleading sometimes. Despite the official policy to abandon the traditional caste system, caste is a social reality in Indian everyday life—sometimes more subtle, sometimes quite drastic.

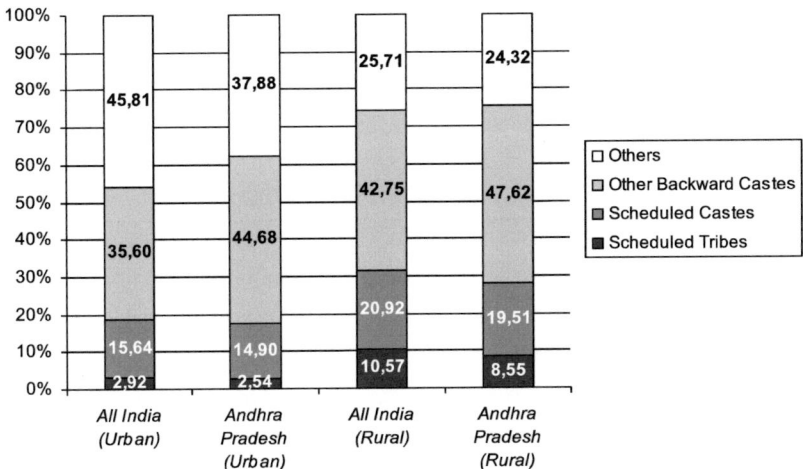

Figure 5: Caste Distribution in Urban and Rural Areas of India and Andhra Pradesh in 2004–05

Source: GoI NSS (2007: 36)

---

[16] While from an European perspective a 7-8 % growth rate seems unrealistically high, the situation is different for India. The Indian economy did grow with a rate of 5.8 % annually in the period 1995–2000, and with a rate of 6.8 % in the 2000–2005 period. In 2005, 9 % have been reached. The Planning Commission of the Government of India assumes an annual growth rate for the current 11th Five Year Plan (2007/08-2011/12) of 9 percent. Andhra Pradesh's growth targets according to this plan are 9.5 % (4 % in the agricultural sector, 12 % in industry, and 10.4 % in the service sector) (Dholakia 2009).

Official statistics account for the Scheduled Castes (SCs), Scheduled Tribes (STs), Other Backward Castes (OBCs) and other caste groups called 'Others' (see Figure 5). For historical reasons, in India these social groups differ with respect to mean as well as distribution of economic welfare, however measured. For instance, in India SCs and STs constitute the socially vulnerable and economically backward classes (Suryanarayana 2008).

While statistical evidence is hard to find, one can—as a zero hypothesis backed by anecdotical evidence—assume that the group of 'Others' shows large overlaps with the middle classes (and the upper class as well), while the class of 'deprived' (in MGI's language) can be found predominantly among scheduled castes and tribes, as well as Other Backward Castes.

India is a democracy, as has often been mentioned. Democracies, among other things, link social interests much closer to the political system than non-democratic regimes. In a democratic country with a majority of poor people, policies do have to address the interests of the poor—at least rhetorically and during election periods, and vis-à-vis the 'vote banks' of the poor quarters. The attempt of many middle class members to 'bypass' politics in order to pursue their interests does also reflect a perceived bias towards the lower strata of society. A more critical assessment of the middle class lifestyle has lately even been approved by the Prime Minister.

> *The time has come for the better off sections of our society–not just in organised industry but in all walks of life–to understand the need to make our growth process more inclusive; to eschew conspicuous consumption; to save more and waste less; to care for those who are less privileged and less well off; to be role models of probity, moderation and charity. (...) The electronic media carries the lifestyles of the rich and famous into every village and every slum. Media often highlights the vulgar display of their wealth. An area of great concern is the level of ostentatious expenditure on weddings and other family events. Such vulgarity insults the poverty of the less privileged, it is socially wasteful and it plants seeds of resentment in the minds of the have-nots. (Singh 2007)*

This evidently points to recognition of intensifying socio-economic inequalities and the role of consumption practices in making such inequalities visible.

For our project we will have to take the social differentiation of Hyderabad into account, e.g. for the sampling process and the issues raised in the household survey, but also when it comes to design pilot projects and policy recommendations. If they are to have an impact, they will have to reflect the different meaning systems and social contexts of different social groups in the city.

7 Stakeholders relevant to Lifestyle and Consumption

Besides understanding the social differentiation in Hyderabad, it is crucial to take into account the vast number of organisations, be it governmental or non-governmental organisations, actors from the private sector, from the science as well as from the media. From all these sectors, we have identified nine important organisations that work from national level; ten from Andhra Pradesh state level, yet based in Hyderabad, and 37 of the identified organisations are directly engaged in Hyderabad. India is well known for its strong civil society engagement and this picture is reflected in the Hyderabad context, too. We have identified a number of 18 non-governmental organisations—most of them directly engaged in Hyderabad, and by some means associated with one of the project's fields of interest. Given this huge number of actors with a link to the project's objectives, it becomes clear how important it is to conduct a comprehensive stakeholder analysis that is able to appraise the power of relevant stakeholders, their interests related to the project's objectives, their potential role in the project and finally their potential interest for cooperation with other stakeholders.

For this purpose, the categorisation and differentiation of stakeholders represents a powerful tool for this evaluation and serves as the basis for any participation planning process. The results are given in Table 1, with a very high information content listing all identified stakeholders categorised by sector and hierarchy level. It comprises all ratings given by the researchers' team with respect to the three dimensions of power, the relevance of climate change for the organisation, the actual and potential role for climate change mitigation and adaptation respectively, their interests in the fields of energy, food/health, and transport/mobility, and their potential role for proposed pilot projects and policy advisory. The power was rated with numbers between 1 and 5, with 5 representing the highest and 1 representing the lowest amount of power. The interest in the three areas of energy, food/health, and transport/mobility either give a positive ("yes") or a negative ("no") statement. All other categories are rated in dots, with black dots rating high or rather significant, grey rating medium, and white rating little or insignificant.

The table provides a comprehensive database that not only serves as the basis for the further promotion of stakeholder participation for the research and development project, but it can also be utilised from all work packages as an information base for their own interactions with stakeholders. An important information drawn from this analysis is the significant weight of the topic of energy compared to the other two fields of interest. Thirty-six stakeholders are interested in the field of energy, while only twenty-three put a focus on transport/mobility, and only twenty are interested in food and health. This sampling is of course biased towards the research interests of sub-project.

Table 1: Categorisation and differentiation of identified stakeholders

Organisation/Institution	Political power	Market power	Network power	Aggregate power	Relevance of climate change for the organisation	Actual role for climate change mitigation	Potential role for climate change mitigation	Actual role for climate change adaptation	Potential role for climate change adaptation	Interest in the field of energy	Interest in the field of food and health	Interest in the field of transport	Pilot project role	Policy advisory role
Governmental Organisations														
PM's Council on Climate Change	5	4	4	13	●	●	●	●	●	yes	yes	yes	○	●
Bureau of Energy Efficiency (BEE)	4	4	2	10	◐	●	●	◐	◐	yes	no	no	○	○
Ministry of New and Renewable Energy (MNRE)	4	3	2	9	◐	●	●	◐	◐	yes	no	no	○	○
Ministry of Urban Development	4	4	2	10	◐	◐	●	◐	●	yes	no	yes	○	○
Department of Consumer Affairs	4	4	2	10	◐	◐	●	◐	●	no	yes	no	○	●
The Consumer Affairs, Food and Civil Supplies Department of the Government of Andhra	4	3	3	10	◐	●	●	◐	●	no	yes	no	○	●
Andhra Pradesh Energy Department	4	3	3	10	○	○	●	○	◐	yes	no	no	○	○
Andhra Pradesh Electricity Regulatory Commission (APERC)	3	4	3	10	○	○	●	○	◐	yes	no	no	○	●
Andhra Pradesh Pollution Control Board (APPCB)	4	3	3	10	◐	◐	●	○	◐	no	yes	no	○	●
Andhra Pradesh Forest Department (APFD)	3	2	2	7	◐	◐	●	○	◐	no	no	no	○	◐

Organisation/Institution	Political power	Market power	Network power	Aggregate power	Relevance of climate change for the organisation	Actual role for climate change mitigation	Potential role for climate change mitigation	Actual role for climate change adaptation	Potential role for climate change adaptation	Interest in the field of energy	Interest in the field of food and health	Interest in the field of transport	Pilot project role	Policy advisory role
Andhra Pradesh National Green Corps (APNGC)	4	2	3	9	◐	◐	●	◐	●	yes	yes	yes	●	◐
Greater Hyderabad Municipal Corporation (GHMC)	5	3	4	12	○	○	●	○	●	yes	yes	yes	○	●
Hyderabad Metropolitan Development Authority (HMDA)	5	4	3	12	○	○	●	○	●	yes	no	yes	○	●
Hyderabad Metropolitan Water Supply and Sewage Board (HMWSSB)	3	2	3	8	◐	◐	◐	◐	●	no	yes	no	○	◐
GHMC City Managers Training Centre	3	1	3	7[17]	○	○	◐	○	◐	no	no	no	○	●
Non-Governmental Organisations														
Energy Conservation Mission, The Institutions of Engineers (India)	3	2	4	9	●	●	◐	●	◐	yes	no	yes	●	●
Forum for Sustainable Development of Hyderabad (FSD)	3	1	3	7	●	●	◐	●	◐	yes	yes	yes	●	●
Forum for a Better Hyderabad (FBH)	3	1	3	7	●	●	◐	○	◐	yes	yes	yes	●	●
Tarnaka Residents Welfare Association	2	2	2	6	●	○	◐	○	◐	no	no	yes	●	●
The Right to Walk Foundation (TR2W)	2	1	2	5	●	●	◐	○	○	no	no	yes	●	●
Campaign for Housing and Tenurial Rights (CHATRI)	2	1	2	5	○	○	◐	○	◐	yes	yes	no	●	○
Confederation of Voluntary Associations (COVA)	2	1	2	5	○	○	◐	○	◐	no	yes	no	●	○
Geoecology Energy Organisation (GEO)	2	2	3	7	●	●	◐	●	◐	yes	no	no	●	●
Non-Conventional Energy and Environment for Rural and Urban (NEERU)	1	2	3	6	●	●	◐	●	◐	yes	no	no	●	●

Organisation/Institution	Political power	Market power	Network power	Aggregate power	Relevance of climate change for the organisation	Actual role for climate change mitigation	Potential role for climate change mitigation	Actual role for climate change adaptation	Potential role for climate change adaptation	Interest in the field of energy	Interest in the field of food and health	Interest in the field of transport	Pilot project role	Policy advisory role
Small-Scale Sustainable Infrastructure Development Fund (S3IDF)	1	2	3	6	○	●	◐	○	◐	yes	yes	no	●	○
Hyderabad Unplug	1	1	2	4	●	●	◐	○	◐	yes	yes	no	●	○
Greenpeace India	1	1	3	5	●	●	◐	○	◐	yes	yes	yes	○	●
Hyderabad Climate Alliance	1	1	2	4	●	●	◐	○	◐	yes	no	no	●	○
Indian Youth Climate Network (IYCN)	2	1	2	5	●	●	◐	○	◐	yes	no	yes	●	○
Organisation for Industrial, Spiritual and Cultural Advancement, OISCA-International	1	1	2	4	●	●	◐	●	◐	no	yes	no	●	○
MMTS (Multi Modal Transport Services) Travelers Group	1	1	2	4	○	●	◐	○	○	no	no	yes	●	○
Winrock International-India	1	1	3	5	●	●	◐	○	◐	yes	yes	no	●	●
The Climate Group India	1	2	3	6	●	●	◐	○	◐	yes	no	no	●	●
Private Sector														
Confederation of Indian Industry (CII)	3	3	4	11	○	●	◐	○	◐	yes	no	no	○	●
Andhra Pradesh Central Power Distribution Company Ltd. (AP-CPDCL)	2	2	3	7	○	○	◐	○	◐	yes	no	no	○	○
Andhra Pradesh Transmission Corporation (APTRANSCO)	3	3	3	9	○	○	◐	○	◐	yes	no	no	○	○
Andhra Pradesh Power Generation Corporation (APGENCO)	3	2	3	8	●	●	◐	○	◐	yes	no	no	○	●
Non-Conventional Energy Development Corporation of Andhra Pradesh (NEDCAP)	3	2	3	8	●	●	◐	○	○	yes	no	no	●	●
Shri Shakti Alternative Energy Ltd.	1	2	2	5	●	●	◐	○	◐	yes	no	no	●	●

Organisation/Institution	Political power	Market power	Network power	Aggregate power	Relevance of climate change for the organisation	Actual role for climate change mitigation	Potential role for climate change mitigation	Actual role for climate change adaptation	Potential role for climate change adaptation	Interest in the field of energy	Interest in the field of food and health	Interest in the field of transport	Pilot project role	Policy advisory role
Adapt Technology (Consultancy in Urban and Regional Planning)	2	1	3	6	○	○	◐	○	◐	no	no	yes	○	●
Green Homes Group (Real Estate Developers)	1	2	1	4	○	○	◐	○	◐	yes	no	no	○	○
HSBC Bank India (The Hong Kong and Shanghai Banking Corporation Ltd.)	1	3	2	6	●	●	◐	○	◐	no	no	no	○	○
SEW Infrastructure Ltd. (Formerly SEW Constructions Ltd.)	3	4	3	10	○	●	◐	○	◐	no	no	yes	○	○
Emaar MGF Land Ltd. - Sustainability Excellence Centre	1	2	2	5	●	●	◐	●	◐	yes	no	no	●	●
Science														
The Energy and Resources Institute (TERI)	2	2	4	8	●	●	◐	●	◐	yes	yes	yes	●	●
Indian Institute of Management, Ahmedabad (IIMA)	1	1	3	5	●	●	◐	●	◐	yes	yes	yes	○	●
Osmania University, Faculty of Social Science (Sociology, Geography, Political Science, Public Administration, Economics)	3	1	4	8	○	○	◐	○	◐	no	no	no	○	●
The Climate, Energy and Sustainable Development Analysis Centre (CESDAC)	1	1	2	4	●	●	◐	●	◐	yes	yes	no	○	●
Engineering Staff College of India (ESCI): Centre for Climate Change, A Forum of The Institutions of Engineers (India)	3	4	4	11	●	●	◐	○	◐	yes	no	no	●	●

Organisation/Institution	Political power	Market power	Network power	Aggregate power	Relevance of climate change for the organisation	Actual role for climate change mitigation	Potential role for climate change mitigation	Actual role for climate change adaptation	Potential role for climate change adaptation	Interest in the field of energy	Interest in the field of food and health	Interest in the field of transport	Pilot project role	Policy advisory role
Centre for Media Studies (CMS)	1	1	3	5	●	○	◐	○	◐	yes	no	no	○	●
Environment Protection Training & Research Institute (EPTRI)	2	1	3	6	●	●	◐	○	◐	no	yes	no	○	●
Centre for Economic and Social Studies (CESS)	2	1	2	5	●	○	◐	○	◐	no	no	yes	●	●
Media														
TV9 – For a better Society	2	2	3	7	○	○	◐	○	◐	no	yes	yes	●	○
Newspaper 'Eenadu' (Telugu)	3	2	4	9	●	○	◐	○	◐	no	no	no	●	○
Newspaper 'The Hindu' (English)	3	3	4	10	●	○	◐	○	◐	no	no	no	●	○

Another important tool for the stakeholder analysis is the power vs. interest mapping that is directly based on the results given in Figure 6. It locates stakeholders according to their power by also taking into account common interests with the overall project. Four categories of stakeholders are differentiated, 'players' who have both an interest and significant power; 'subjects' who have an interest but little power; 'context setters' who have power but little direct interest; and the 'crowd' which consists of stakeholders with little interest or power (see Figure 6).

---

[17] Refer to GHMC.

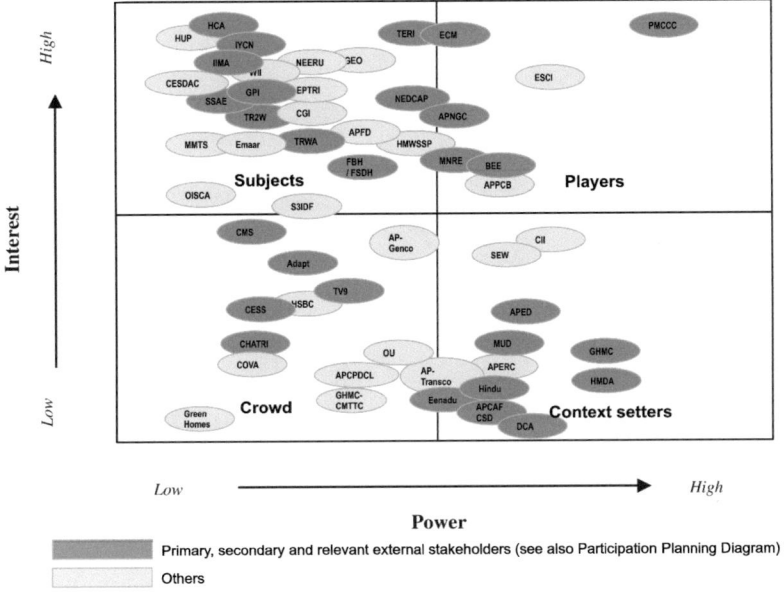

Figure 6: Results of power vs. interest mapping

Source: Based on Bryson (2004: 30)

Against the background of the huge number of stakeholders and the resulting complexity, it was difficult to derive any valuable information from the map given above. Therefore, we developed a further step to reduce complexity and increase specificity. Three separate maps were drawn with regard to the respective interest groups[18], vis. energy, transport/mobility, and/or food. This visualisation helps to identify the most appropriate stakeholders for each field of interest, it highlights potential for stakeholder cooperation based on common interests, and—most importantly—it visualises the common interest groups according to their power and their interest with the objectives of the project. These maps were then discussed within the team of researchers by again taking into account the qualitative information data base to chose a selection of primary, secondary and tertiary (external) stakeholders. This represents a subset of all the stakeholders we screened, and focuses on those we would like to work with in the near future. As mentioned, stakeholder analysis is an ongoing activity, so that changes might occur during the course of the project. The results are given in Figure 7, 8, and 9.

---

[18] Interest here refers to an interest in one of the three topics energy, transport/mobility, and/or food. It does not consider the interest on the project's objectives to e.g. reduce GHG emissions in Hyderabad.

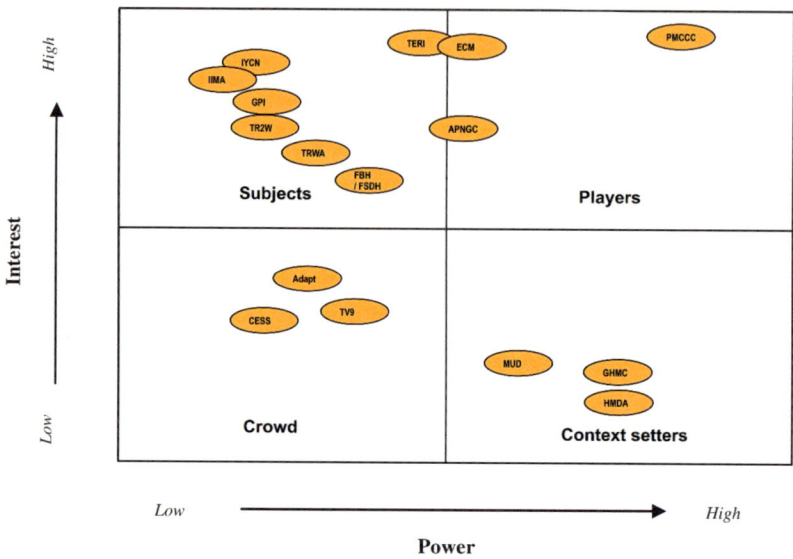

Figure 7: Stakeholders with interest in transport and mobility

Source: Based on Bryson (2004: 30)

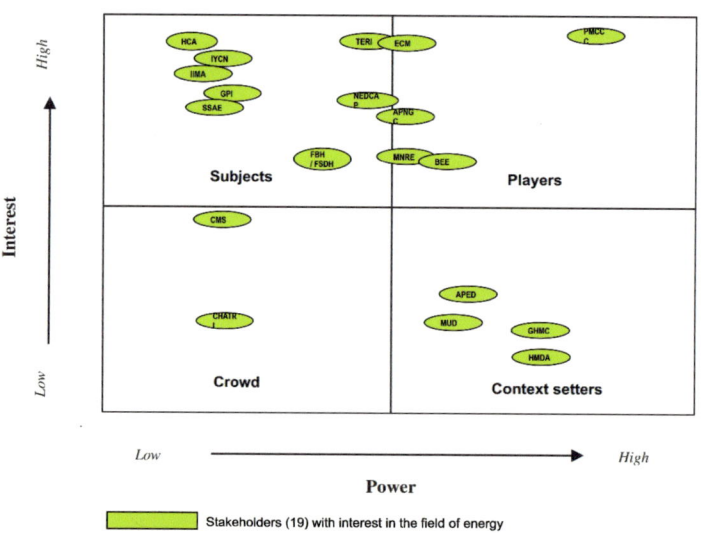

Figure 9: Stakeholders with interest in energy

Source: Based on Bryson (2004: 30)

Based on the foregoing steps a participation-planning diagram was developed comprising all those stakeholders that appear functional for any of the project's objectives.

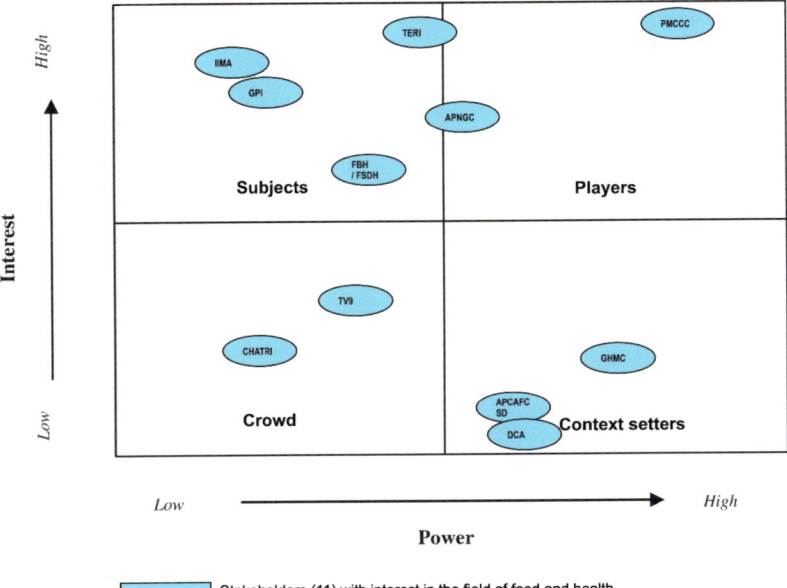

Figure 8: Stakeholders with interest in food and health
Source: Based on Bryson (2004: 30)

The stakeholder map serves as an approximation to delineate potential participation and cooperation with respect to the project implementation, mediated from the results of the categorisation process. It depicts stakeholders from different sectors such as governmental organisations, NGOs, civil society organisations, private sector, media, and science. Governmental organisations are separated on national, state, and urban administration level while the other stakeholders are not further differentiated.

Central target group are the lifestyle groups viz. upper class, middle class and the urban poor. Important stakeholders that may have a strong influence on the target group are the NGOs, most of them being based in Hyderabad. Here, it is necessary to differentiate between primary and secondary stakeholders. Primary stakeholders (highlighted in dark grey) are those who are expected to play a leading role during the process of the project as major facilitators of change. Five out of seven primary stakeholders are NGOs, while the other two represent the science (TERI) and the administration of Hyderabad (GHMC). Secondary stakeholders (highlighted in light grey) rather play a subsidiary role through either connection to key stakeholders or through their indirect influence in the field of lifestyle change and energy consumption. However, secondary stakeholders are likely to become primary stakeholders through the process of the project. All other relevant stakeholders (distinguished in white) are important for the project's objectives as they may be able to set boundary conditions, but—through their rather external character (e.g. with their position on national administrative level)—they are fairly out of reach to be influenced through the project's contributions in Hyderabad. In following, the major areas of interest for the promotion of stakeholder participation will be delineated along the basic structure of the stakeholder participation diagram.

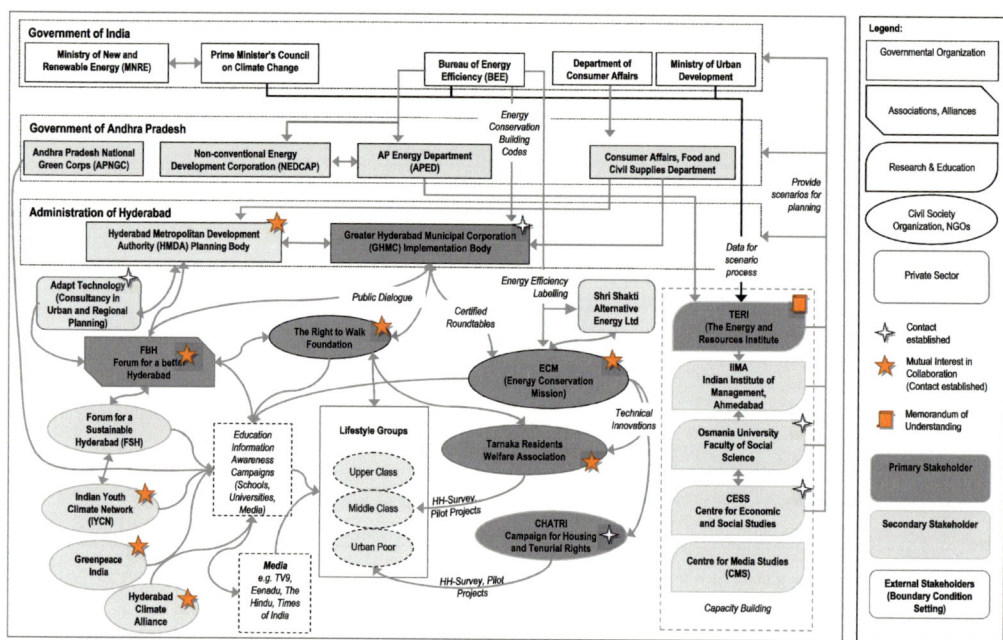

Figure 10: Stakeholders with interest in energy
Source: Own draft

The promotion of sustainable lifestyles in Hyderabad with the focus on climate change mitigation and energy use is among the core objectives. There is a considerable number of local NGOs and civil society organisations located in Hyderabad that directly or indirectly pursuit some or the other aspect of the major objective targeted by the sub-project. NGOs and civil society organisations generally apply citizen-oriented approaches and hence suit well for the purpose of targeting consumers on household level. Therefore, we have identified a number of promising actors from the NGO sector that are most likely to promote the objectives of the overall project driven from their own impetus together with the support of the project.

The scenario process is another important objective. The development of energy scenarios for the city of Hyderabad has to be understood as an iterative process that aims to address and involve a wide set of actors not only from science but also from government. Data input and advisory from relevant government organisations on national, state and municipal level will not only increase validity of underlying data, but also contribute to relevance and ownership of the results for successful promotion of a sustainable development pathway. The results of the scenario process will ideally disseminate back to all involved government stakeholders for an application in planning.

The promotion of Capacity Building is another important component engaging the science to target urban local government bodies as well as NGOs and the private sector. Capacity Building for us comprises guidance and assistance in conducting household surveys as well as implementing pilot projects in the study areas (Tarnaka Residents Welfare Association, CHATRI). Capacity Building will also play a significant role in mainstreaming the promotion of sustainable consumption and climate change mitigation mediated through the NGO community as well as the mass media.

8 Outlook for the Stakeholder Participation Process

This report builds on a comprehensive desk research analysing structure and positions of local, regional and national stakeholders that might be relevant for a transition of Hyderabad into a low-carbon megacity. Although the study also considers a few assertions given by key informants in the course of preliminary, explorative expert interviews conducted in Hyderabad and Delhi, our conclusions predominantly reflect the views and assumptions of the German research team. Therefore, it is necessary to further integrate stakeholders' perspectives into the analysis and to understand it as an iterative process throughout the ongoing course of the project. For this purpose it was an important aim of this study to emphasise on a visualisation of the analysis process and its results in order to build a strong basis for promoting stakeholder participation in the future. The stakeholder maps and diagrams are a good starting point to discuss and amend stakeholder positions and relations in concert with local experts and primary and secondary stakeholders. Only together with these stakeholders it is possible to propose and plan their potential role and contributions to the project. The participation-planning diagram highlights certain roles and contributions of identified key stakeholders, but—intentionally—only on the surface. In an intercultural context and given the complexity of a megacity, only through stakeholder participation it is gainful to (a) formulate problems adequately and (b) to create ideas for locally adjusted strategic interventions. Both have to be developed through the process of stakeholder interaction in well planned, concerted workshops and sessions in Hyderabad—and, above all, by planning, organising and evaluating concrete (pilot) projects. This will also connect and empower key stakeholders with high interest in the projects' objectives, but little power ('subjects') to exert their influence.

For instance—with regard to the promotion of sustainable transport in Hyderabad, solutions from other countries or cities such as Singapore are likely to fail due to the unique social-cultural and physical conditions in Hyderabad. One of the key identified stakeholders in this area is represented by *The Right to Walk Foundation (R2WF)*, initiated by a group of dedicated people who were unsatisfied with the given situation and who are well-aware of the local conditions and institutional constraints. R2WF promotes a pedestrian friendly city through campaigns, petitions, and the constant dialogue with staff from the *Greater Hyderabad Municipal Corporation (GHMC)*. R2WF is also a member of an alliance called *Forum for a Better Hyderabad (FBH)* that also serves as a mouthpiece for the initiative. Both, R2WF and FBH are primary stakeholders. Taking Figure 7 into consideration, it becomes clear that there are certain other stakeholders interested in the field of transport and mobility with partly quite different objectives. R2WF has already established personal links to the GHMC and the FBH, but still lacks power and influence to fully achieve its goals.

In fact, a large number of stakeholders *do* rate sustainable development and the improvement of quality of life in the city high on their agenda. We therefore assume that there is a huge potential for cooperation and to involve a larger number of stakeholders with high interest in our project's objectives. Stakeholder workshops and seminars that also serve as a platform for Capacity Building on the topic of climate change mitigation and sustainable urban development will contribute to an exchange of positions, ideas and experiences. Such meetings will also be instrumental to facilitate cooperation among stakeholders with common interests. We are confident that the promotion of stakeholder communication and cooperation will help to form a critical mass at least in the NGO community of Hyderabad.

Getting other stakeholders to the table, especially those with power and little interest is more challenging. However, given the established contacts to the GHMC and the

Hyderabad Metropolitan Development Authority (HMDA), it is likely that it will be possible to organise workshops also together with staff from the municipal government level, but also from the private sector. This is not only due to the fact that—as an international research project—we have a quotable name in Hyderabad. Ideally, many stakeholders will rate it as prestigious to collaborate with the BMBF sponsored project from Germany. Moreover, we gather a significant number of contacts from various sectors and hierarchy levels. We also provide an information data base with a huge number of contacts in Hyderabad and beyond and stakeholders are likely to utilise our contacts for strategic networking.

Some of the pilot projects we would like to initiate in the next phase reflect this. Together with the Energy Conservation Mission (ECM), we plan to organise certified round-table workshops for the city's administration and business corporations in order to mainstream energy conservation and climate issues for their daily operations.[19] Together with other Work Packages of the project and stakeholders in Hyderabad, we plan to substitute inefficient and indoor-polluting stoves in poor quarters for more energy efficient and local income generating stoves, either based on solar energy or on biomass. Together with the Tarnaka Residential Welfare Association (TRWA), the Right to Walk Foundation (TR2W), the city's traffic administration and PTV we would like to design pilot projects for integrated traffic management and increased share of environmentally friendly mobility.[20] Together with Human Geography Freiburg and local partners we want to integrate climate and energy issues into a modernised food retailing system at a quarter level. Together with partners form the local government (APNGC), NGOs, selected schools and the mass media we plan to develop campaigns for awareness rising in adaptation and mitigation issues for different lifestyle groups in the city.

In summary, the stakeholder process serves both interests, stakeholders gain through an additional platform for networking and their discourse. What is even more important, our scientific data and background knowledge through Capacity Building will provide stakeholders new effective argumentation patterns for their strategic discursive actions. They can draw on our produced knowledge in order to effectively participate in the local and higher level economic, urban development and climate change discourse. Ideally, this will improve their positions on the basis of our argumentation. In this way we exert

---

[19] ECM is in the position to certify these round tables and has already done so in the past. Together with our project, the link to climate policy will become more explicit.

[20] Greater Hyderabad Municipal Corporation (GHMC) is participating in ICLEIs (Local Governments for Sustainability) Cities for Climate Protection (CCP) Campaign, where traffic projects are going on.

our influence on the discourse. Assuming a best case scenario, we thereby facilitate the process of an evolving local discourse on climate change and we will be able to directly involve in the development of dispositives such as new or adjusted institutions, acts and laws, reports and documents as well as pilot projects that focuses on clean energy use, sustainable lifestyle, public transport solutions and in general climate change mitigation and adaptation.

The great benefit for the German research project gained from the stakeholder analysis process is the learning from the stakeholders about local conditions, problems, local institutions and constraints, new contacts, actors' relationships, power relations and most important locally developed and adjusted solutions. We moreover learn how to participate in the local discourse on climate change and other related areas and we *do* actively participate.

As Hyderabad has really been a 'testing ground for governance reforms since the 1990s (Kennedy 2006), we are looking forward to co-operate with various stakeholders in a network kind of approach. Having distinguished between four basic types of capacity building (cf. Chapter 2), we now feel better prepared to deal with the various stakeholders involved, especially with respect to their different positions with respect to power and interest.

References

Ahmad, Imtiaz and Reifeld, Helmut (eds.). 2002. *Middle Class Values in India and Western Europe*. New Delhi: Social Science Press.

Béteille, André. 1996. "The mismatch between class and status". *British Journal of Sociology* 47(3): 513–525.

Béteille, André. 2001. "The Social Character of the Indian Middle Class." In *Middle Class Values in India and Western Europe*. Imtiaz Ahmed, and Helmut Reifeld, (eds.), 73–85. New Delhi: Social Science Press.

Bhalla, Surjit S. 2004. "Not as Poor, Nor as Unequal, as You Think: India, 1950–2000." Report on research project entitled *The Myth and Reality of Poverty in India*. New Delhi: Planning Commission, Government of India.

Bhushan, Chandra, Mario D'Souza, Sunita Narain, Pratap Pandey, Pradip Saha, and Singh Yadav. 2008. "A Curtain Raiser on the Climate Negotiations in Poznan, Poland." *Down To Earth, Science and Environment Online* 18(14), www.downtoearth.org.in [12-05-2009].

BJP (Bharatiya Janata Party). 2009. Party Manifesto for the Lok Sabha Elections 2009. www.bjp.org/content/view/2844/428 [10-05-2009].

Botzen, W. J. W., J. M. Gowdy, and J. C. J. M. van den Bergh. 2008. "Cumulative CO_2 Emissions: Shifting International Responsibilities for Climate Debt." *Climate Policy* 8: 569–576.

Bourdieu, Pierre. 1987. *Distinction: A Social Critique of the Judgement of Taste*. Cambridge, MA: Harvard University Press.

Bryson, John M. 1995. *Strategic Planning for Public and Nonprofit Organizations*. San Francisco, CA: Jossey-Bass.

Bryson, John M. 2004. "What to Do When Stakeholders Matter? Stakeholder Identification and Analysis Techniques." *Public Management Review* 6(1), 21–53.

Cohen, Stephen P. 2001. *India: Emerging Power*. New Delhi: Oxford University Press.

CPI (Communist Party of India). 2009. *Party Manifesto for the Lok Sabha Elections 2009*. http://allindiapeoplesmanifesto.files.wordpress.com/2009/04/cpi-manifesto-20091.pdf [10-05-2009].

CPI/M (Communist Party of India, Marxist). 2009. *Party Manifesto for the Lok Sabha Elections 2009*. http://cpim.org/manifesto.pdf [10-05-2009].

Das, Samantak, Dripto Mukhopadhyay, and Sanjib Pohit. 2005. "Mitigating Carbon Emission through Economic Instruments: An Indian Perspective." NCAER Working Paper 050001, National Council of Applied Economic Research. www.ncaer.org/Downloads/WorkingPapers/WP96.pdf [12-05-2009].

Derné, Steve. 2008. *Globalization on the Ground: Media and the Transformation of Culture, Class, and Gender in India*. Los Angeles etc.: Sage.

Deshpande, Satish. 2003. *Contemporary India: A Sociological View*. New Delhi: Penguin Books.

Dholakia, Ravindra H. 2009. "Regional Sources of Growth Acceleration in India." W.P. No. 2009-03-06, Ahmedabad: Indian Institute of Management.

Dittrich, Christoph. 2009. "The "New" Middle Classes in India's Hightech Capital Bangalore: Between Abundances and Squeeze." In *Globalizing Lifestyles, Consumerism, and Environmental Concern – The Case of the New Middle Classes*. Helmuth Lange, and Lars Meier, L. (eds.). Berlin etc.: Springer.

Eden, C. and F. Ackermann. 1998. *Making Strategy: The Journey of Strategic Management*. London: Sage.

Fernandes, Leela. 2006. *India's New Middle Class: Democratic Politics in an Era of Economic Reforms*. Minneapolis: University of Minnesota Press.

Fernandes, Leela. 2007. "The Political Economy of Lifestyle: Consumption, India's New Middle Class and State-led Development". Paper presented at the Workshop on *Globalizing Lifestyle. Between McDonaldization and Sustainability Perspectives: The Case of the 'New Middle Classes'*, University of Bremen, October 4–5, 2007.

Freeman, R. E. 1984. *Strategic Management: A Stakeholder Approach*. Boston, MA: Pitman.

Fuller, Chris, Haripriya Narasimhan. 2007. "Information Technology Professionals and the New-Rich Middle Class in Chennai (Madras)." *Modern Asian Studies* 41(1): 121–150.

Gadjil, Madhav, Ramachandra Guha. 1995. *Ecology and Equity: The Use and Abuse of Nature in Contemporary India*. New York: Routledge.

Ganguly, Sumit (ed.). 2003. *India as an Emerging Power*. London: Frank Cass.

GOI (Government of India). 2008. *National Action Plan on Climate Change*. New Delhi.

GOI NSS (Government of India, National Sample Survey Organisation). 2007. *Household Consumer Expenditure among Socio-Economic Groups: 2004-2005 NSS 61st Round (July 2004-June 2005)*. Report No 514 (61/1.0/7). New Delhi: National Sample Survey Organisation, Ministry of Planning and Programme Implementation.

GTZ (Deutsche Gesellschaft für Technische Zusammenarbeit). 2001. *Mainstreaming Participation: Instrumente zur Akteursanalyse*. Eschborn: Deutsche Gesellschaft für Technische Zusammenarbeit (GTZ).

Harriss, John. 2005. *Middle Class Activism and Poor People's Politics: An Exploration of Civil Society in Chennai*. Development Studies Institute Working Paper 72. London: London School of Economics.

Hust, Evelin. 2005. "Introduction: Problems of Urbanization and Urban Governance in India." In *Urbanization and Governance in India*. eds. Evelin Hust, and Michael Mann, Michael, 1–26. New Delhi: Manohar.

Hust, Evelin, Michael Mann (eds.). 2005. *Urbanization and Governance in India*. New Delhi: Manohar.

IEA (International Energy Agency). 2006. *CO_2 Emissions from Fuel Combustion 1971–2004*. Paris: Organisation for Economic Cooperation and Development (OECD).

INC (Indian National Congress). 2009. *Party Manifesto for the Lok Sabha Elections 2009*. www.congress.org.in/manifesto09-eng.pdf [15-05-2009].

IPCC (Intergovernmental Panel on Climate Change). 2007. *Climate Change, The Synthesis Report*. Geneva. IPCC. www.ipcc.ch/pdf/assessment-report/ar4/syr/ar4_syr.pdf [12-05-2009].

Jackson, Tim. 2008. "The Challenge of Sustainable Lifestyles." In *State of the World 2008. Innovations for a Sustainable Economy*. (ed.)Worldwatch Institute, 45–60. Washington, DC: Worldwatch Institute.

Jenkins, Rob. 1999. *Democratic Politics and Economic Reform in India*. Cambridge: Cambridge University Press.

Jepsen, Anna Lund, and Pernille Eskerod. 2009. "Stakeholder Analysis in Projects: Challenges in using current Guidelines in the real World." *International Journal of Project Management* 27: 335–343.

Jha, Raghbendra. 2007. "Vulnerability of Consumption Growth in Rural India." *Economic and Political Weekly* 24: 711–715.

Johnson, G., K. Scholes. 2002. *Exploring Corporate Strategy*. Harlow: Pearson Education.

Joseph, Kurian. 2006. "Stakeholder Participation for Sustainable Waste Management." *Habitat International* 30(4): 863–871.

Kalam, Abdul, Y. S. Rajan. 1998. *India 2020: A Vision for the New Millennium.* New Delhi: Viking.

Kapur, J. C. 1982. *India: An Uncommitted Society.* New Delhi: Vikas Publishing House.

Kaschub, Thomas. 2007. "A GIS Based Enterprises Inventory for Technical Infrastructure Planning in the Fast Growing City of Hyderabad in India." Karlsruhe: Institute for Industrial Production (IIP).

Kelkar, Ulkar, and Suruchi Bhadwal. 2007. "South Asian Regional Study on Climate Change Impacts and Adaptation: Implications for Human Development." Human Development Report 2007/2008. Fighting Climate Change: Human Solidarity in a Divided World. Human Development Report Office, Occasional Paper.

Kennedy, Loraine. 2006. "Decentralisation and Urban Governance in Hyderabad. Assessing the role of different actors in the city." Hyderabad: CESS, GAPS Series, Working Paper No. 8.

Kettl, D. 2002. *The Transformation of Governance: Public Administration for Twenty-First Century America.* Baltimore, MD: Johns Hopkins University Press.

Kolli, R. K., K. Krishna Kumar, R. G. Ashrit, S. K. Patwardhan, and G. B. Pant. 2002. "Climate Change in India: Observations and Model Projections." In *Climate Change and India: Issues, Concerns and Opportunities.* (eds.) P. R. Shukla, S. K. Sharma, and Ramana P. Venkata. New Delhi: Tata McGraw-Hill Publishing Company Limited.

Kothari, Rajni. 1974. *Footsteps into the Future: Diagnosis of the Present World and a Design for an Alternative.* New Delhi: Orient Longman.

KPMG. 2008. *Climate Change. Is India Inc. Prepared?* A KPMG Study.

Kumar, K. S. K. 2004. "Climate Change Impacts on India." In *India and Global Climate Change: Perspective on Economics and Policy from a Developing Country.* (eds.) Michael A. Toman, Chakravorty, and Shreekant Gupta. New Delhi: Oxford University Press.

Kumar, Naveen, and Suresh Chang Aggarwal. 2003. "Patterns of Consumption and Poverty in Delhi Slums." *Economic and Political Weekly* 13: 5294–5300.

Mawdsley, Emma. 2004. "India's Middle Classes and the Environment." *Development and Change* 35(1): 79–103.

Merton, Robert K. 1995. "The Thomas Theorem and the Matthew Effect." *Social Forces* 74(2): 379–424.

MGI (McKinsey Global Institute). 2007. *The 'Bird of Gold': The Rise of India's Consumer Market*. San Francisco: McKinsey & Co.

Mistry, Dinshaw. 2004. "A Theoretical and Empirical Assessment of India as an Emerging World Power." *India Review* 3(1): 64–87.

Myers, Norman, and Jenniver Kent. 2003. "New Consumers: The Influence of Affluence on the Environment." *Proceedings of the National Academy of Sciences* 100(8): 4963–4968.

Münch, Richard. 1996. *Risikopolitik*. Frankfurt am Main: Suhrkamp.

Nilekani, Nandan. 2009. *Imagining India: The Idea of a Renewed Nation*. New Delhi: Penguin.

Nutt, P., and R. Backoff. 1992. *Strategic Management of Public and Third Sector Organizations: A Handbook for Leaders*. San Francisco, CA: Jossey-Bass.

O'Brien, Karen, Robin Leichenko, Ulka Kelkar, Henry Venema, Guro Aandahl, Heather Tompkins, Akram Javed, Suruchi Bhadwal, Stephen Barg, Lynn Nygaard, and Jennifer West. 2004. "Mapping Vulnerability to Multiple Stressors: Climate Change and Globalization in India." *Global Environmental Change* 14: 303–313.

Oommen, T. K. 2004. "Futures India: Society, Nation-State, Civilisation." *Futures* 36: 745–755.

Parikh, Jyoti, and Kirit Parikh. 2004. "The Kyoto Protocol: An Indian Perspective." *International Review for Environmental Strategies* 5(1): 127–144.

Powell, W. 1990. "Neither Market nor Hierarchy: Network Forms of Organization." In *Research in Organizational Behavior*.: (eds.) B. Staw, and L. Cummings. Greenwich, CT: JAI Press.

Rajni, Bakshi. 1998. *Bapu Kuti: Journeys in Rediscovery of Gandhi*. New Delhi: Penguin Books.

Reed, Mark S., Anil Graves, Norman Dandy, Helena Posthumus, Klaus Hubacek, Joe Morris, Christina Prell, Claire H. Quinn, and Lindsay C. Stringer. 2009. "Who's in and why? A Typology of Stakeholder Analysis Methods for Natural Resource Management." *Journal of Environmental Management* 90: 1933–1949.

Reusswig, Fritz. 2009. "Lifestyle Dynamics as a Means of the Sustainability Transition: A Systems Perspective." In *Sustainable Production and Consumption Systems*. (eds.) L. Lebel, and S. Lorek. Cheltenham: Edward Elgar.

Reusswig, Fritz, Antonella Battaglini. 2008. "Lebensstildynamik als Katalysator einer nachhaltigen Energiewende." In *Wege aus der Klimafalle. Neue Ziele, neue Allianzen, neue Technologien – was eine zukünftige Klimapolitik leisten muss.* (eds.) H. E. Ott, and Heinrich-Böll-Stiftung, 162–188. München: Oekom-Verlag.

Reusswig, Fritz, Antje Otto, Lutz Meyer-Ohlendorf, and Ulrike Anders. 2009. "Climate change discourse in India: an analysis of press articles" (Additional Study). Berlin, Potsdam.

Roy, Joyashree. 2006. "The Economics of Climate Change. A Review of Studies in the Context of South Asia with a Special Focus on India." Report Submitted to The Stern Review on the Economics of Climate Change. Kolkata. www.hm-treasury.gov.uk/d/roy.pdf [12-05-2008].

Singh, Manmohan. 2007. "Ten Point Social Charter." Speech delivered at the Confederation of Indian Industry, 24 May 2007. www.mbauniverse.com/innerPage.php?id=ne&pageId=326 [20-05-2008].

Shukla, P.R., Subash Dhar, and Dipitranjan Mahapatra. 2008. "Low-Carbon Society Scenarios for India." *Climate Policy* 8: 156–176.

Sridharan, E. 2004. "The Growth and Sectoral Composition of India's Middle Class: Its Impact on the Politics of Economic Liberalization." *India Review* 3(4): 405–428.

TERI. 2009. "An Exploration of Sustainability in the Provision of Basic Urban Services in Indian cities." TERI in partnership with Sustainable Urbanism International and Arghyam, with support from Rohini and Nandan Nilekani. New Delhi: TERI Press.

ToI (Times of India). 2008. "India ready with Climate Action Plan." 29.6.2008.

UNDP. 2007. *World Population Prospects: The 2007 Revision.* http://esa.un.org/unup [19-05-2009].

Upadhya, Carol. 2004. "A New Transnational Capitalist Class: Capital Flows, Business Networks and Entrepreneurs in the Indian Software Industry." *Economic and Political Weekly* 39(48): 5141–5151.

Varma, Pavan K. 1998. *The Great Indian Middle Class.* New Delhi: Viking.

Veblen, Thorstein. 1899. *The Theory of the Leisure Class: An Economic Study of Institutions.* London: Allen & Unwin.

World Bank. 2008. *World Development Report 2008.* Washington, DC: The World Bank.